by keith ferrazzi

Leading Without Authority

Who's Got Your Back

Never Eat Alone

leading without authority

leading without authority

HOW THE NEW POWER OF
CO-ELEVATION CAN BREAK DOWN
SILOS, TRANSFORM TEAMS, AND
REINVENT COLLABORATION

KEITH FERRAZZI

with NOEL WEYRICH

CURRENCY
NEW YORK

Published in the United States by Currency, an imprint of Random House, a division of
Penguin Random House LLC, New York.

CURRENCY and its colophon are trademarks of Penguin Random House LLC.

Library of Congress Cataloging-in-Publication Data

Names: Ferrazzi, Keith, author.
Title: Leading without authority / Keith Ferrazzi.
Description: First edition. | New York: Currency, [2020] | Includes bibliographical
references and index.
Identifiers: LCCN 2020003080 (print) | LCCN 2020003081 (ebook) |
ISBN 9780525575665 (hardcover) | ISBN 9780593138694 (international) |
ISBN 9780525575672 (ebook)
Subjects: LCSH: Leadership. | Organizational behavior. | Management—
Employee participation.
Classification: LCC HD57.7 .F4726 2020 (print) | LCC HD57.7 (ebook) |
DDC 658.4/092—dc23
LC record available at lccn.loc.gov/2020003080
LC ebook record available at lccn.loc.gov/2020003081

Printed in the United States of America on acid-free paper

crownpublishing.com

2 4 6 8 9 7 5 3 1

First Edition

Book design by Jo Anne Metsch

*To the new generation of leaders young and old
who are co-creating a new definition
and meaning of leadership*

contents

leading without authority

THE NEW WORK RULES FOR A NEW WORK WORLD

Nothing gets done in a single silo or function anymore. Constant collaboration is at a new premium, because the big things are always led by cross-functional teams. We need people driven by purpose, passion, and persistence, not position or job title. We need people who will seek out the right solution and then figure out how to get a team together to build it. It's no longer about hiring great talent. It's about hiring talent that will make the team great.

BRIAN CORNELL, CEO, Target

We live in a momentous time in human history, one that has never offered more abundance and opportunity. But these times have also brought about a Category 5 hurricane of disruptive changes. Breathtaking advances in science and exponential technological innovation bloom all around us, making our lives better and easier. And yet there are people at all levels of organizations who feel fatigued, fretful, and even beaten down at work. It's a Dickensian dichotomy—the best of times and the worst of times.

Everywhere I go, I hear a litany of lamentations. In a given week I may coach executive teams at a medical products company in Japan, a global bank in New York, an aerospace contractor in Los Angeles, or a hedge fund in Moscow. The complaints I hear are all the same. Outwardly, they touch upon turf battles, budget brawls, and organizational constraints, but they are heartfelt, born of real fear of personal failure.

Many are quick to blame the mounting pressures caused by technology. But I disagree. This era of explosive change has merely exposed the built-in flaws and unsound footing of how we have always worked. Even at companies that extol values like inclusion and collaboration on their websites and breakroom walls, I hear a similar beleaguered sentiment echoing up and down the chain of command. Executives, managers, and front-line associates alike bemoan their less-than-productive relationships with colleagues in the midst of disruption and transformation.

We are long overdue for a change in the way we work. Advancing technology has made that change an urgent necessity.

> The idea that every employee in an organization must lead without authority is one of the most exciting and challenging realities in American business today. At Farmers I imagine the creative power of 20,000 employees, representing 20,000 life experiences and literally millions of insights, versus the natural limitations of a C-level leadership team of six or eight "leaders with authority." These changes can be liberating if we embrace them, so that innovation and transformation are no longer the responsibility of a few leaders or teams, but instead represent opportunities for every employee.
>
> JEFF DAILEY, president and CEO, Farmers Group, Inc.

THE LIMITATIONS OF AUTHORITY

When I was a young entry-level consultant at Deloitte in the 1990s, straight out of business school, I quickly discovered I wasn't cut out for building spreadsheets and crunching numbers. The work I was assigned left me feeling restless and bored, so I filled my off-hours doing things that were more interesting to me and, I felt, more beneficial to Deloitte. I made calls to ex-classmates, professors, and old employers to tell them all about my new employer and ask them for new leads. I booked myself as a speaker at small conferences all around the country on weekends, hoping to generate buzz and drum up business for Deloitte. I even organized a new business quality award in Illinois that advanced the state's economic agenda while helping connect Deloitte Partners to regional business leaders.

The result? My first-year review was a humiliating experience I'll never forget. I just wasn't holding up my end of my assigned duties. But my supervisors saw promise in my hobby of generating new business for the firm. They decided to give me an expense account and set me loose to keep promoting Deloitte full-time, the same way I'd been while off the clock.

In less than a year, I had developed an informal marketing function at Deloitte. With no one reporting to me and no real authority, I simply engaged everyone related to marketing that I could. I never let a title (or my lack of one) stop me. Early on, I asked to have dinner twice a year with Pat Loconto, Deloitte's CEO at the time. During those meals, I did my best to be my authentic self, offering him my candid advice in the spirit of being of service to him and his legacy.

By leading without authority, I was determined to make an impact at Deloitte as we built a global brand name in the consulting business. I wasn't willing to wait ten years (typical at the time) to be anointed for some kind of leadership position. Instead, I built critical relationships with influencers inside and outside the company, and went on to become Deloitte's chief marketing officer (CMO) and later its youngest-ever partner.

In 1994 I left Deloitte to become global CMO at Starwood Hotels—making me the youngest CMO at any Fortune 500 company at the time. This role, working with CEO Barry Sternlicht, gave me full authority over the marketing resources for *all* the company's divisions around the world. Together, we created a powerful global suite of brands that offered a consistent experience to our guests, no matter where they were. Over time, we consolidated Starwood's marketing resources, all in service of efficiency and global consistency, the same as our Deloitte team had done.

There was one person who fought my centralized authority. Starwood's head of Europe insisted that he and his marketing people were far better suited to decide where and how to spend Starwood's European marketing budgets. It was true that he knew the market more intimately, but my mandate was to invest in the global brand. We collaborated on European marketing, but he had to relinquish the control he would have liked.

Then Starwood's global president moved on, and guess who replaced him? Starwood's head of Europe. It wasn't long before I found my CMO position gutted, with most of my budget dispersed to marketing heads in regional divisions across the globe. My job was set to become a hollowed-out shell of what it had been; I was heading out the door.

It took some time for me to process what I learned from that defeat. Looking back, it became clear that once I had a title and authority at Starwood, I set aside many of the leadership traits that had earned me the job in the first place. I had excelled at leading without authority. I was a natural at it. But once I had some authority of my own, I didn't spend as much time building strong relationships as I had at Deloitte. I'd assumed that my new global role would give me and my team the authority to achieve great things. I felt I was on a mission, blessed by Starwood's CEO, and I was going to see that mission all the way through. Or so I thought.

In 2004, while working as a CEO for a start-up, I began writing my first book, *Never Eat Alone*.[1] It was a smash hit, a bestselling guide to creating opportunities and developing relationships by connecting with people through generosity, authenticity, and vulnerability—just as I had done at Deloitte. By then, as an entrepreneur, I was maintaining thousands of VIP and influencer relationships (including a few with some extremely challenging people), and I wanted to share my recipe for success with everyone.

Around that time, I launched my own consulting firm, Ferrazzi Greenlight (FG). Our mission? To transform the collaborative nature of teams to accelerate organizational growth. (Today, I just say we transform teams to transform the world.) We've made a science out of building high-performing cross-functional teams committed to breakthrough innovation. Some of the world's most successful business leaders, largest nongovernment organizations, and even some governments have hired us during times of disruption to reboot their behaviors and cultures to make them nimbler and more innovative than their competitors.

Through my decades of team coaching, I've come to see how many people are repeating the same mistakes I made at Starwood so many years ago. Too many managers rely on their title, position, and budgetary control to get their work done. They waste too much of their energy on painful bureaucratic infighting, energy that would be better spent leading others to collaborate and seek audacious new solutions. And I find that people without formal authority are often sitting on the sidelines, waiting their turn, when they could be diving in as I did at Deloitte, building relationships and leading without authority to get extraordinary things done.

Employers *need* us to seize opportunities, take the initiative, and build value for our companies. Sclerotic old-school command-and-control decision-making is no longer going to cut it. A 2016 survey of HR professionals by my old employer Deloitte found that just 24 percent of large companies with fifty thousand or more employees are relying on functionally organized hierarchies to get work done. "Organizations," the report said, "are shifting their structures from traditional, functional models toward interconnected, flexible teams."

The report continued:

> The entire concept of leadership is being radically redefined. The whole notion of "positional leadership"—that people become leaders by virtue of their power or position—is being challenged. Leaders are instead being asked to inspire team loyalty through their expertise, vision, and judgment.[2]

Leading without authority has never been more important, and the need for it grows more urgent by the day. The consulting group Gartner predicts that by 2028, algorithms will eliminate so many middle-management jobs that work will depend almost entirely upon networks of cross-functional teams. Gartner describes them as "ensembles of autonomous and high-performing teams delivering crucial outcomes."[3]

Klaus Schwab, one of my early mentors and the founder of the World Economic Forum, writes that we are now in a "Fourth Industrial Revolution," which, he says, is so complex and fast-moving that it demands a new type of leadership that "empowers all citizens and organizations to innovate, invest and deliver value in a context *of mutual accountability and collaboration.*"[4]

> At Zappos, company culture is our #1 priority. We believe that employees have so much more potential than most companies (and even the employees themselves) realize, and it's just a matter of putting them in the right context. I'm excited to bring "co-elevation" as a book, as a concept, and as a new word to Zappos to help create that context and bring our culture to the next level.
>
> TONY HSIEH, CEO, Zappos.com

THE NEW WAY FORWARD

Leading without authority is unavoidably becoming *the* twenty-first-century organizational model. The trouble is that for most managers, the secret to applying the model reliably and with excellence remains a mystery. The Deloitte survey revealed that although cross-functional teams are held in high regard, "just 21 percent feel expert at building cross-functional teams, and only 12 percent understand the way their people work together in networks."[5] That's not going to get it done.

The old rules of the game aren't working anymore. But every day I still see people clinging to those old rules by their fingertips. Why? Because there are no rules to the new game we're playing, and no manual for how to play the game well.

Until now.

This book is the first to codify a new set of work rules for our new work world. It gives readers a complete, holistic, and proven methodology for succeeding in a world in which the ability to lead without authority is an essential workplace competency.

The solutions I prescribe in this book call for awakening to a new understanding of leading without authority and applying to that mindset a new workplace operating system that I call co-elevation.

Simply defined, *co-elevation* is a mission-driven approach to collaborative problem-solving through fluid partnerships and self-organizing teams. When we co-elevate with one or more of our associates, we turn them into teammates. We enter into close co-creative relationships based on candid feedback and mutual accountability. With its guiding ethos of "going higher together," co-elevation nurtures a generosity of spirit and a sense of commitment to our new teammates and our shared mission. The resulting outcomes almost always exceed what could have been accomplished through regular channels within the org chart.

Think of co-elevation as your road map for thriving in uncertain times and dealing with the tremendous disruptive pressures afflicting every industry. Each rule and technique for co-elevation in this book is aimed at fostering a new workplace organizing principle, one in which each employee leads one or more informal teams toward greater success outside the lines of hierarchy. Leading without authority through co-elevation requires many of the personal qualities and practices I first set out in *Never Eat Alone:* generosity, gratitude, vulnerability, forgiveness, and celebration.

I believe co-elevation is capable of transforming even the most contentious workplace relationships into mutually beneficial partnerships. When we co-elevate, we work with more positive energy, generate more innovative ideas, expand our abilities, and execute faster. Though these ideas might sound naive to some, our work at Ferrazzi Greenlight has proven that these are the personal qualities that are absolutely necessary to thrive in the new work world. Our work has shown how candid, trusting relationships based on mutual accountability within teams lead to better sales, more productivity, greater innovation, deeper engagement, and, ultimately, increased revenues, profits, and shareholder value—all in the face of unpredictable forces of disruption and an unprecedented pace of change.

Since getting my MBA, I have been an entry-level employee, a Fortune 500 executive, an entrepreneur, a start-up founder, and a CEO. I wish I'd had this book to read at every one of those career mileposts. For midlevel and senior managers, co-elevation can reinvigorate our outlook and produce breakthrough results across all kinds of silos and chains of command that are strangling performance. For up-and-comers with little or no formal managerial responsibilities, co-elevation can serve as an indispensable toolkit for demonstrating their leadership abilities. For entrepreneurs, co-elevation opens up new possibilities for teamwork that can expand their vision for their company. In the C-suite, co-elevation can be a powerful new model for collaboration and cooperation at the top of the company—one that can build a movement of behavioral change throughout the organization.

Co-elevation will help leaders, teams, and organizations at every level cut through bureaucratic bottlenecks of authority and achieve better, faster results. As you co-elevate with others, you can begin to take on new transformative missions with your expanded teams, collaborating to achieve goals you never would have imagined before.

My goal is to enable you to wield co-elevation like a superpower, extending your reach and accomplishments far beyond the limits and boundaries of your assigned responsibilities. Practicing co-elevation will give you a leg up in your career and in your life. That is how powerful these principles are. You'll be like Superman walking under Earth's yellow sun.

In the coming pages, I will show how to deploy this superpower to exceed expectations within your organization—whether you work for a nimble, high-growth start-up, a privately owned company, a charitable nonprofit, or a global corporation.

Leading Without Authority is the product of more than a decade of research, observation, and testing by our coaches, consultants, and PhD researchers at FG, working with some of the world's greatest transformational leaders. The rules, practices, and prescriptions appearing in this book owe so much to the insights and experiences of the hundreds of executives my team and I have worked with and supported, and the countless associates we have served.

In the research for this book, I have interviewed over a hundred CEOs and leaders I've been privileged to meet and work with. And you will hear from them firsthand throughout the book, offering their own advice and experiences with these new work rules.

Honestly, I've been inspired watching them respond and adapt to the exponential pace of change that has engulfed the economy and their businesses. I am often in awe at their passion and determination to learn, to grow, and to be better leaders. This book would not exist without their insights and contributions.

Companies of all sizes are discovering that co-elevation can achieve organizational objectives that otherwise would languish in the dead spaces between departments and divisions. The simple truth is that every employee, from the mailroom to the C-suite, can be a leader by using co-elevation to recruit like-minded allies in their efforts.

I've seen the results in companies from Minneapolis and Detroit to Milan and Dubai. Dozens of Fortune 500 companies have relied on FG to help them foster far-reaching change and unlock billions of dollars in revenue growth and shareholder value. General Motors, with more than 180,000 employees, has adopted many of the core tenets of co-elevation while turning around its huge North America division. Dun & Bradstreet's CEO and his executive team embraced co-elevation to assist the company's solutions across once impenetrable silos. The result was a 20 percent stock price lift in that year.

We've also introduced co-elevation to leaders at Silicon Valley start-ups, including Box, Dropbox, Lyft, DocuSign, Uber, Zoom, and Coinbase, among others. As these young companies scale and grow, they have a unique opportunity to bypass outmoded organizational structures entirely and organize instead as fluid networks of cross-functional co-elevating teams.

And co-elevation is contagious. By its design, it compels us to keep enlisting more and more people to our cause, creating a bias toward action and innovation. Co-elevation transforms organizations through *personal* transformation. It calls for everyone within an organization to exercise leadership in collaborative partnerships, regardless of their title or position. The relentless pressure to innovate demands co-elevation, because opportunities arise too fast to be dealt with any other way.

> The digital revolution is lowering the bar-to-entry for competition in all businesses. Old organizational structures that require "permission from your boss" before you participate on a project or initiative can't survive. Leading without authority provides the essential way forward. It shows the path to being nimble and forming collaborative partnerships, no matter what the title or position.
>
> SCOTT SALMIRS, CEO, ABM

TIME FOR A WORKPLACE REBOOT

In times of stress, people in charge tend to fall back on familiar ways of managing, so change of this kind needs to start with each of us. Growing up, I saw firsthand the pain workers experienced when management resisted keeping up with changes in the marketplace. It's a pain etched in my heart, from seeing my steelworker father laid off time and time again, putting our family in financial peril as cheaper and higher-quality products from Japan flooded the US market in the 1970s and 1980s.

My dad would often return from the factory grumbling about all the wasteful and inefficient practices on the floor, and how his foreman ignored him whenever he tried to make helpful suggestions. It wasn't his place to say anything, he was told, and he was even advised at times to slow down his pace because he was showing up the slower workers and making the foreman look bad. So many of the problems in the US steel industry (and the auto industry it supplied) were obvious to my dad; he had a front-line vantage point. But management's shortsightedness resulted in my dad losing his job, like thousands of other workers in the factory towns of Western Pennsylvania.

It didn't seem fair to me. Even as a small boy, I felt determined to do something about it. Encouraged by my father, I studied hard and got full scholarships to two of the best private schools in the country. I went on to Yale and when I graduated in 1988, I didn't head off to Wall Street like so many of my peers. I was the only Yale graduate that year to get a job in manufacturing. I wanted to figure out how to help families like my own.

I became an expert in Total Quality Management, which uses the principles of worker-empowered teamwork and continuous improvement to achieve higher levels of quality. I was on the factory floor, assisting workers like my dad to innovate and develop solutions. This quality movement, which I was part of in its early years, did indeed help American business in the 1990s regain the competitive footing it had lost twenty years before.

Well, here we go again. The time has come for yet another big reboot in the workplace. And I believe you're holding the guidebook to that reboot in your hands. What if instead of feeling bogged down by relentless pressure at work, we felt uplifted? What if we excelled not through self-sacrifice, but through mutual self-care? What if those holding us back instead had our backs? What if our sources of stress were transformed into sources of power through collaborative partnerships?

The good news is that so many answers to the challenges facing business are readily available but untapped, just as they were in my dad's day. Leading without authority is hardly a new idea. President Dwight D. Eisenhower, the supreme commander of the Allied forces in Europe during World War II, defined leadership as "the art of getting someone to do something because he wants to do it."[6] I believe in a similar concept called "finding your teammate's blue flame," which I describe on page 81.

In the coming pages, you'll learn how to build co-elevating relationships and how to develop your own co-elevating teams. You'll get a step-by-step guide in how to reinvent collaboration in the workplace in a way that is bold and inclusive, and generates radically improved outcomes. You'll see the power of co-development, a peer-to-peer coaching methodology that fulfills co-elevation's promise to "go higher together." You'll see the importance of gratitude, praise, and celebration with new eyes. And you'll see how sparking a workplace movement that draws on co-elevation can lead to a worldwide movement for reimagining how we all show up with each other in the world.

As in *Never Eat Alone*, I offer a lot of tips, strategies, and suggestions, knowing that not every point will apply or appeal to everyone. Consider the many suggestions in this book not as to-do lists, but as a resource kit. Try one suggestion, then try another, to see what works best for you. In tough times, it can be tempting to hunker down just when the situation calls for opening up. You'll learn through these practices how to resist the urge to fall back on your authority within the organization and top-down control, and instead join with others to achieve what, in fact, can only be done together.

The coming chapters feature stories about people at different stages of their careers, from entry-level positions to CEOs, and in different industries. Don't get distracted by the story specifics and attempt to dismiss them as not applicable to you. It pains me to think I might fail to reach you as a reader because an individual I profile doesn't exactly reflect your situation. Stretch a bit to see yourself and your own circumstances in each of the examples. The principles of co-elevation are just that: universal principles that apply to everyone in the workplace and beyond.

The stories of triumph and travail told in this book have been included with the permission of the people involved. In many instances, I have used pseudonyms and masked key details to disguise people's identity. My intent is to empower, not embarrass those who—like all of us—have tripped up at times and made mistakes. People's interactions can be messy, and as you will see, the stories of co-elevation are not always pretty or flattering. I have made countless mistakes personally and have embarrassed myself enough to attest that failure is a natural part of learning to co-elevate.

It takes time, effort, patience, and practice to develop a successful co-elevating relationship. Honestly, it's a new way of showing up every day, one that requires new ways of thinking, communicating, and behaving. In that sense, this book is a prescription for a healthier workstyle. And just as when you adopt a healthier lifestyle and commit to a new diet and exercise, you won't get it right all the time. I sure haven't, and neither have the people whose stories I share throughout the book. Sometimes you'll say the wrong thing at the wrong time. You may think you've earned permission to offer candid feedback to someone on your team when you really haven't.

There will be times you may think you're being vulnerable and open or empathetic when others don't experience it that way. My advice? Just stick with it. It's a North Star to shoot for, a journey, not just a destination, with plenty of challenges and setbacks along the way.

> In today's rapidly changing environment, we must constantly transform across organizations and as leaders to stay relevant. This requires massive acceleration of innovation, leading with compassion, and making fast, bold decisions. It is so important to consistently remove obstacles so that our teams can better collaborate together to achieve success and make a positive impact on the world.
>
> CHUCK ROBBINS, chairman and CEO, Cisco

WORKING WITH GRAVITY

I believe passionately in co-elevation. I believe the spirit of co-creation unlocks human potential—in service to better ourselves, to better each other, to better our organizations, and to help address even the largest global problems.

I have come to apply co-elevation in every aspect of my life. It's a standard of behavior that I try to bring to being a parent, to building friendships, and to finding my soul mate. Co-elevation has the power to inspire and motivate people in very deep and personal ways. People tell me they've incorporated its principles in their social lives, in their romantic lives—even into their wedding vows. One day a friend texted me an image of a tattoo he'd just put on the inside of his wrist: "coelevate," it said, in simple lowercase Times New Roman font. He did it to honor his bride and set a standard for the most important relationship of his life. His text read, "You've permanently marked me, my friend."

Those of us who are first to adopt co-elevation as a personal ethos will gain a critical advantage. This holds true across all industries, at all levels of government, as well as in nonprofit groups, colleges and universities, and hospitals. I feel confident that in five or ten years, any enterprise that fails to embrace these practices will find itself struggling to stay relevant. If you are stuck doing things the old way, the clock is ticking. A gigantic shakeout is coming, and the winners will be those organizations nimble enough to have transformed their workplace cultures and the people working within them.

Futurist Ray Kurzweil writes that the actual impact of technological change over time is *exponential*, not linear, "so we won't experience 100 years of progress in the 21st century—it will be more like 20,000 years of progress (at today's rate)."[7]

The coming years will be marked by transformational disruption unlike anything we've seen before. It's an exciting time to be alive. Author Peter Diamandis has written that the future is one of abundance. Technology, he says, is a "resource-liberating mechanism. It can make the once scarce now abundant." Abundance, from Peter's perspective, is not about providing everyone with lives of luxury. "Rather," he writes, "it's about providing all with a life of possibility."[8]

Peter is a world-renowned scientist and entrepreneur, the founder and chairman of the XPRIZE Foundation, and a co-founder of Singularity University, where I am a behavioral science faculty member. I'm fortunate to count him as a dear friend and partner, and he considers me his collaborative transformation coach. The vision of the future that Peter sees with such clairvoyant wisdom will not come about without a fundamental co-elevating shift in our behavior toward our work and toward each other. In order to enjoy, in Peter's words, lives of possibility amid the "once scarce now abundant" fruits of change, we must cast off all the grasping scarcity-based behaviors encouraged by the rigid silos and chains of command of the old work world. Peter counts on me and my work to inform that behavior change.

I use the expression "working with gravity" to allude to the basic drivers behind our intrinsic human nature. We all thirst for belonging. And that need provides great opportunity for *any* leader, with or without authority. Since the dawn of time, the rationale for being a member of a tribe is survival, both individual and collective. Our lives improve when we contribute to the collective welfare of the tribe, when we co-elevate. Co-elevation is part of our DNA.

I founded Ferrazzi Greenlight on this same principle. We started our research into the behaviors that drive organizational growth nearly twenty years ago. I told our team that one of our most important design principles would be to look into things that humans are fundamentally hardwired to do. Thus, my shorthand: "working with gravity." When reviewing a prospective practice or technique, I would ask my team, "Are we working with or against gravity on this?"

So here is my final note before we begin: When we practice co-elevation, we are working with a force as strong and durable as gravity itself. We are all hardwired for co-elevation. Even those among your teammates who may seem uncooperative are awaiting your invitation to co-elevate, to co-create, to co-develop. The wind is at your back.

Again, co-elevation is a superpower that can help you and those around you do heroic and amazing things. It is a power within us all. Every one of us, whatever our title, can be a better, more effective, more influential, and more engaged leader. But only you can take the first step. As you'll learn in the following chapters, it's all on you.

WHO'S YOUR TEAM?

> Position does not define power—impact defines power. Impact can be made in every role at every level, and when we prioritize bringing out the best in those around us, business growth and success follow. We're at a critical time where deeply held notions about work are rapidly evolving. We must cultivate diverse workplaces where space is created for honest and constructive feedback and where associates further each other's success. In short, we need to build organizations that value and encourage co-elevation.
>
> MINDY GROSSMAN, CEO, WW International

S andy was exhausted and angry. "Taking this job was a huge mistake," she told me. "The corporate politics here are ridiculous. It's like *Game of Thrones,* but without the chivalry."

The HR director for a national bank in Chicago, Sandy was dealing with problems dumped on her that were beyond her authority to fix. Her biggest challenge was a companywide project she was heading that would centralize HR's control of pay incentives throughout the organization. Not long after Sandy launched the initiative, she and her boss caught wind of a plan by the sales department to implement its own bonus incentive program.

Sandy's boss worried that HR would look bad if other departments followed the sales department's example and set up similar independent bonus programs. If that happened, HR's centralized program would almost certainly fail to meet its projected cost savings. But her boss didn't want to confront the head of sales on the issue, so he laid the problem at Sandy's feet. He asked her to persuade Jane, the head of sales operations and the department's second-in-command, to drop the sales bonus plan. "Nip it in the bud," he told Sandy.

Sandy lacked the authority to tell Jane what to do, so she wasn't surprised when Jane responded flat out that the department needed its own targeted bonus system to remedy its soft fourth-quarter sales results. Sandy was left in an impossible position. She lacked the authority to force the sales department to comply with the new HR initiative, and her boss would be angry if the initiative failed.

Sandy was one of the best young executives I knew. I had met her several years earlier during work FG had done with her previous employer. She reached out and asked me to have lunch before a talk I was giving in Chicago to a group of HR leaders, and I gladly accepted. A few others I'd invited to join couldn't make it, so it ended up being just me and Sandy.

Before our meal arrived, Sandy set down her iced tea and confided that she was thinking of looking for a new job. "I just don't know if I'm cut out for this place," she said. She had earned this job, with its big title and salary, by being a good leader who always took care of her staff. They knew she had their backs; that's why she was so naturally adept at getting more from them than anyone expected.

As frustrated as Sandy was with Jane, she also felt victimized and abandoned by her boss for his refusal to confront the head of sales over the issue. Her complaints sounded all too familiar to me. Politics within an organization can be extremely demoralizing and create a victim mentality in even the ablest people. I had certainly felt victimized at Starwood when the new president took away my budget authority as CMO.

But I had a question for Sandy. "Are you *absolutely certain* that your companywide bonus program is the best answer for sales? Will your program help sales make their quarter?"

Sandy admitted that she couldn't be sure, but that it wasn't really her first concern. It was sales's responsibility to make its numbers, which it had repeatedly failed to do, and Sandy had enough problems of her own. She'd also been charged with leading a cross-functional team to develop a mobile app for HR, and that project was running behind. People from other departments critical to the app's design and launch kept missing her meetings. It was another instance of people outside her chain of command threatening to undermine projects that she would be held accountable for.

HOW'S YOUR TEAM?

I asked Sandy, "How's your team doing?"

"My people are as frustrated as I am," she said. "You know me. I try to protect them as best I can."

I asked her again, "Yes, but how's your *team*?"

Sandy smiled, familiar with my coaching methods. "What's the game, Keith? I just told you how they are."

"I'm telling you this as someone who cares deeply about you and your career," I said. "The team you're failing is the team you don't even realize exists."

"Okay," she said cautiously. "What team are you talking about?"

"Your team," I told her, "is made up of *everyone* who is critical to helping you achieve your mission and goals."

Like nearly all managers, Sandy saw her team as her direct reports within the org chart. But Sandy faced far too many obstacles in getting her work done to take such a limited view of her leadership responsibilities. The only way to overcome all those obstacles successfully was for Sandy to embrace the notion that her team was a much larger network of people, far beyond the HR employees she was assigned to supervise.

That was the difficult proposition I had for Sandy. Could she inspire that same team commitment and performance among people over whom she had no authority? More specifically, could she engage with the sales department as though they were members of her own team, with the same sense of common purpose and shared desire to find solutions?

My goal in our conversation was to help shift Sandy's mindset away from seeing herself as a victim, and instead see herself as a leader of a larger team. Every workplace suffers from office politics. The remedy is to lead a team of your own creation. To lead others who do not necessarily report to you. In other words, to lead without authority.

And that's the foundation of Rule One of the new work rules. You must awaken to the realization that for every goal you have, for every project or mission you have, you are responsible for leading a much broader group of people than the formal members of your team. The more ambitious the mission, the broader this group will be, and yet your leadership of this group must be as committed as it would be if each one of them were reporting to you.

Most of us feel a sense of loyalty and obligation to the formal teams we are assigned to, or that are assigned to us. We care about the people on our teams—at least, on good days. We support them and go to bat for them; we want them to succeed and grow. Now, as the work continues to shift toward more loosely organized cross-functional teams, we have to extend that same degree of care, concern, commitment, and camaraderie to *all* our new team members—even the people we don't yet realize are on the team. It's the only way to achieve extraordinary results.

LOST IN THE MATRIX—ON STEROIDS

Sandy's situation illustrates how common it is today for managers to have accountability, but without full control. Sandy was accountable for rolling out the new bonus pay program, but she didn't control the other departments' compliance with her program.

She was also accountable for the HR mobile app project, but couldn't compel members outside her formal reporting team to attend her meetings. Likewise, Jane and the people in sales were accountable for making their quarterly numbers, but HR was threatening to take away control of the bonus program sales managers needed to motivate their team.

Starting in the 1990s, the emergence of large-enterprise software like SAP and Oracle helped companies save money and exert more direct control from the top down with automated processes in finance, HR, procurement, supply chain, even legal and marketing. Executives and consultants touted the benefits of this increasingly centralized "matrix" structure for global consistency, to reduce costs, to eliminate redundancies, and to streamline procedures. But in the process, divisions and regions lost portions of their autonomy. Tensions naturally arose over questions of control, ownership, and authority—the residue of old, ingrained models of hierarchy.

When the matrix was introduced, an extremely high value was put on collaborating across vertical organizational silos. But the idea was only given lip service. Although everyone was expected to work cross-functionally, the result was no different than working in traditional silos. It was akin to just laying the silos on their sides. As in Sandy's case, these old battles over turf, control, ownership, and authority, initiated with the introduction of the matrix, are still actively waged today.

Traditional work rules, with their misguided ethos of "I must have control to get it done," or "That's not my job," or "He's not my direct report," or "I don't have the authority to do it," haven't caught up with today's new work realities. It's a big reason so many nimble, fast-moving start-ups have so effectively disrupted entire industries, right out from under giant, well-established, matrix-organized industry leaders.

Perhaps the defining characteristic of the new work world is *radical interdependence*. Top-down management still sets the budgets, but the work itself is getting done through these sprawling networks of radically interdependent relationships. No single manager can have sufficient authority, wherewithal, or resources to meet the deluge of today's challenges. In the words of one of my clients, "We need to do work so great that you couldn't possibly do it alone."

Never Eat Alone stressed the vital importance of creating opportunities through authentic, generous, and mutually supportive relationships within your personal network. That's as true today as it was back when the book was published in 2005. But the new work world has added another layer of effort to the equation. Our networks have evolved into the primary medium for getting work done. And because everyone in most organizations is connected through these radically interdependent networks, our effectiveness is ultimately determined by our ability to lead, inspire, and serve our *network*. Think of it as a *network of networks*.

Consider your own work situation. Are you a manager with the sole authority over all the resources you need to get your job done? Or if you work for a manager, does he or she have authority over all the resources needed to be effective? My guess is that if you think you have that kind of authority, then you are likely not thinking big enough about the impact you could be making at your organization. Ask yourself, who are the people you rely on the most to achieve results who are also outside your line of authority? More than likely, you count on many people to get things done, beyond those who are your direct reports or formal teammates. And yet so many of us, whether we are colleagues or managers, remain fixated on "Who is the boss? Who has the authority?"

When we continue to operate under the old work rules, we risk finding ourselves out of step with the times. Every moment we spend focused on gaining more control over resources to get things done is a precious moment wasted. Those are moments better spent building relationships and co-creating with people and resources *outside your direct control.* You'll identify ways to help one another develop new capabilities and gain new perspectives, which will ultimately help you achieve greater things. The age of radical interdependence requires us to engage in these kinds of deeper, richer collaborations with people we often have no control over in order to fulfill our mission and move the organization forward.

In short, we all need to think of ourselves as leaders, as innovators, regardless of our job titles. We all have to demonstrate initiative and encourage deeper collaboration so we can contribute the full range of our ideas and talents to what we do.

> Industry disruption demands unprecedented innovation at a speed and scale that cannot be produced inside traditional organizational boundaries. We need a fundamental mindset shift that embraces the challenge of innovating across boundaries, both inside and outside the company. The future of leadership requires a focus on identifying the right teammates for each project, and then co-elevating to generate novel solutions and extraordinary outcomes.
>
> TAMI ERWIN, executive vice president and group CEO, Verizon Business Group

"WHO IS ON MY TEAM?"

I ask every team that I work with the same question: "Who are the most critical people to help you achieve your goals right now, whether or not they are currently aligned to your org chart?" *These* are the people on your team. No matter who they report to formally in the chain of command, they are all members of the team you need to lead without authority in order to get things done.

Sandy understood immediately what I was asking. The trouble was that she had so many projects going on, she felt overwhelmed by the number of potential teammates she could reach out to.

"So start somewhere," I said. "Select the *one* person absolutely needed for the success of one important project. Start there. Where do you want to start to gain some traction?"

Sandy knew in an instant that that person was Jane in sales. Yet for a host of reasons, attempting to co-elevate—to establish a deeper, caring relationship with this formidable colleague—felt impossible.

For starters, Sandy felt deeply suspicious of Jane, and Jane's behavior did nothing to allay her concerns. Jane withheld information from Sandy and neglected to invite Sandy to meetings in which the sales bonus incentives were discussed and developed. Her actions showed that she didn't want Sandy anywhere near the sales team's project. All of which further fueled Sandy's suspicion of Jane and filled Sandy with resentment.

"You're telling me to treat her as if she were on my team," Sandy said. "Well, if someone is on my team, I support them, take care of them, and direct them. I work to understand their goals and help them achieve them. I do my best to protect them from the bureaucracy and corporate BS, and from pressure from above. You're suggesting I feel and act the same way toward Jane? You're joking, right? She's the corporate BS I need to protect others from!"

I told Sandy I wasn't joking at all. To really pick up the mantle of leadership, Sandy needed to embrace Jane, regardless of her suspicions of her. "Every one of us over our careers has been part of a team with at least one person we're at odds with," I said. "Through the work, we figure out how to make it work. Now you've got to figure out how to make it work with Jane."

I knew that asking Sandy to accept Jane—someone she saw as a dangerous competitor—as part of her team wasn't easy. Sandy and Jane didn't have any shared experiences, which is how we typically create an emotional connection with others. In order to co-elevate with Jane, Sandy would need to build an intimate relationship with her from scratch, which is very difficult.

When the younger of my two foster sons came to live with us, he was twelve. We hadn't conceived him. We weren't there to watch him take his first steps. We hadn't been there to answer the questions of a curious boy or chase after a rambunctious boy. When he came into our lives, we had to make the conscious choice to love him as our son, even though in a fit of rage he often yelled, "You will *never* be my father!" He had been in so many homes before ours—he was not going to let another family raise his hopes, only to dash them again.

It wasn't easy, but I gave all I had to embrace him with love, compassion, and understanding. Because, after all, he *was* now my son. That was my commitment to him—to both of us. I had to be all in. It was going to be tough enough for us all, I knew, and without that level of commitment on my part up front, there could be no hope of a relationship with him or for his growth in our family.

Now I was asking Sandy to step up and embrace Jane, and the rest of her sales team, as *her* team, with a common goal. And there really was a common goal that Sandy and Jane needed to share, one that Sandy could not dispute: They both should take the shared responsibility to help boost the company's revenue.

The reality was, however, that Sandy had yet to embrace that larger picture. Pressure from above had left Sandy so obsessed with the potential of Jane's program to embarrass the HR department that she hadn't given serious thought to whether elements of Jane's plan might, in fact, be more effective at increasing sales.

"Nobody wins if the sales team loses," I told Sandy. "Isn't there a shared mission between you and Jane to find a way to use the compensation plan to drive revenue growth and innovate against your competitors? Doesn't that mission deserve full consideration? You haven't worked with Jane and her team to scope out better solutions."

I encouraged Sandy to treat Jane the same way she would a new report, someone she wanted to make feel welcome. I knew that was something Sandy was always good at. I suggested she approach Jane with the following mindset: "How can I serve you in creating a bonus program that will improve your team's performance in the coming quarter? One that will keep costs in line, increase revenues, and strengthen the company as a whole?"

Once Sandy was able to view Jane and the entire situation from a more dispassionate perspective, she began to see the opportunity before her. "Perhaps," she said, "we can engineer a bigger win for everyone."

This relationship awakening is the first step in the co-elevating process. You need to come to the table looking to disrupt your own thinking. If you want to achieve an outcome that has a greater impact than what you might have achieved on your own, you have to arrive with a sense of curiosity at the forefront of your mind. Set aside your conviction that your way is the right way. Open yourself to the assumption that others on your team have ideas that may be far better than yours.

Toward the end of that workday, Sandy stopped by Jane's office and, for the first time, spoke with Jane as a teammate. She apologized for being so single-minded in their previous encounters and asked if they could hit reset on their relationship.

Jane began to open up as the conversation progressed. Sandy was surprised to learn that Jane had actually kept Sandy away from the sales team's meetings regarding bonuses not as a power play, but because Jane felt embarrassed by her team's lack of engagement. The sales reps' results were projected to be underwater for that quarter, and Jane was worried that her plan was so far behind schedule, she might not get it completed quickly enough to impact the quarter's results.

Sandy and Jane were in the same boat. By accepting one another as *teammates,* each rid herself of the burden of being defensive and began to spend more time and energy focusing on the real mission at hand.

Over the subsequent days, Sandy worked intensively on the compensation project with Jane and her sales team. With Sandy at the table representing HR, some sales team members were more attentive to the project because they were able to raise other related issues that impacted sales and sales compensation. With HR and sales functioning as one co-elevating team, a divisional bonus program emerged that worked as a complement to HR's centralized system. Other departments copied elements of this new semi-customized program and even added their own innovations. With Sandy's active involvement, elements of each division's plan were shared with the others, transforming the bank's entire incentive pay program and making HR look better than ever before.

Together Sandy and Jane created a completely new system of department-specific incentives at their company. But this transformational result wasn't possible until Sandy was first able to change her concept of who was on her team.

Transformation is an all-hands-on-deck challenge. Winning organizations will be those that achieve broader inclusivity in decision-making and eradicate the idea that "it's not my job." The best, most resourceful workers are those who are able to co-elevate with their team members and engage with whomever is needed to get things done and accomplish the mission. There is no more important skill than to build and lead teams that cut across divisions and functional silos to achieve breakthrough results.

MILIND MEHERE, founder and CEO, YieldStreet

RULE ONE: THE PRACTICES

When we lead without authority, we consider *all* the people who may be critical to us achieving our goals. And we enlist them as members of our team. It's a unique opportunity to set aside the limits imposed by the resources you control, and instead consider the impact you want to make.

But where to start? What's the mission? How can you elevate it? Perhaps you're in sales and want to redesign how you go to market by bringing the product and marketing folks onto your team. Or there's some sort of friction point between your department and another group and your goal is to eliminate it, fixing what hurts most right now, as Sandy did. Every company's leadership needs its employees aiming as high as possible to create breakthrough solutions to meet new market pressures, and the only way to do this is to bring everyone who could contribute to your mission onto the team.

Here are some tips and best practices about how to get started co-elevating, how to build on early success, and how to best track and organize all your co-elevating teams.

Start Where It's Easiest

Leading without authority doesn't have to be hard like it was for Sandy. My advice, early on, is to find someone you think you'll have a positive experience co-elevating with. Choose someone most likely to grasp the roughly outlined vision you think deserves your collective attention. Even better, I would encourage you to start building that co-elevating relationship before you need to. The more time you spend nurturing and building relationship ties with an associate you respect and think you may want to work with on something big, the easier it will be later to invite them to join you in taking on challenging and aspirational projects together.

Then shift your focus toward potential partners and new teammates who can help you to achieve positive momentum fast. Don't waste too much time trying to convince resisters to join the fun. In our coaching of large-scale change, we find that when you build momentum with positive people first, the resisters tend to come around once they start seeing results.

Check Your Hot Button Priority

Sometimes, you have no choice. You need to start building your team in the midst of a crisis, when everyone feels they're behind the eight ball. For Jane and Sandy, there wasn't a lot of time to weigh the potential advantages and pitfalls of working together. They had to try.

So what's stressing you out? What's keeping you up at night? What's occupying your headspace? Where can you introduce the co-elevation conversation as a potential solution? You will likely find, as Jane and Sandy did, that the very urgency of the situation will help you forge the bonds necessary for a productive co-elevating relationship.

Look for Those You Admire and Want to Learn From

On any given day, we bump into extraordinary people who could up our game and make us better at achieving our goals. In the next project meeting, instead of checking email or pondering what you'll say when it's your turn to report, pay attention and take note of who speaks up with the most interesting insights. Is there a project you can imagine co-creating with someone else you admire, not just for the project's impact, but for the learning experience or to deepen the relationship? Does someone have special knowledge or a unique background you could learn from? Do you see someone who is a diamond in the rough, someone you feel is being underutilized by the company, someone who might become really energized if you came to them with an idea? If you are going to initiate real breakthrough ideas, who would be an ideal partner for such a mission? Well, go get them on your team.

Co-elevating with team members who work remotely is a challenge. You have to work a little harder to connect with them. Use conference calls or video calls as a way to introduce yourself to people you want to get to know better. Follow up with them with an individual call or meeting so you can talk without an agenda. I can't tell you how rare it is for a team member on a call to follow up with remote members of the team when it's not required. Take that extra step, and you will stand out.

Identify Someone You Believe Would Benefit from Your Help

All of us work with people who could improve their performance with the right guidance or encouragement. If you are truly committed to a mission or project and you find that someone's performance is holding the group back, why not do what any good leader would do and coach them? Take responsibility for making a positive difference in that person's career so you can make a positive difference toward the project or mission at hand.

When you open channels for discussion, active collaboration, and mutual development, you'll be surprised what can follow. Co-elevating with a teammate not only allows your team to achieve more, it will also help you grow in your own performance and alleviate your own pent-up frustration, which no one needs to hold on to.

Face the Person or Problem You're Avoiding

Admit it—there's a project you're putting off, right? That's true for all of us. Have you been procrastinating? Is the code too hard to crack? Are you terrified of failure? Or is it that you don't know where to begin?

And maybe the problem isn't a something, but a *someone*. Perhaps they're Jedi masters at triggering your emotional hot buttons—or you theirs. Or perhaps you feel at times like you're in an emotional MMA cage battle with them, whether your disagreements are expressed openly or fester under the surface. Well, take that as a sign of a relationship that you can improve, and lean into it. Sometimes, we avoid certain people and projects because they hold an important key to our success. In his essay "Heroism," Ralph Waldo Emerson passed along this bit of received wisdom: "Always do what you are afraid to do."

Be Systematic and Scale

As you get more comfortable with this approach to team-building, you will want to become more systematic about how you use co-elevation to achieve greater scale. As a young executive at Deloitte, I devised a quick and easy system for relationship management that I call the RAP—relationship action plan. I've since taught it to CEOs (as well as a few presidential candidates) and we use it at FG as our tool for designing and managing co-elevating teams.

In the words of management guru Peter Drucker, "What gets measured gets managed." Once you begin co-elevating with several people on several different projects, you'll want to start a RAP for each project or team you're working with. Begin by making a prioritized list of your most critical relationships for the project at hand.

Ask yourself, "What's my goal for this particular RAP?" Take notes and define the specific outcome you hope to create with each member of your co-elevating *team*. Whose support do you need to be successful?

For each project or mission, the initial RAP list should have anywhere between five and ten names on it. With Sandy and Jane, their shared mission was to create the best possible bonus program, one that would help the sales team close more deals, increase revenue, and make the organization more successful. Sandy and Jane put both of their bosses on their RAP. Next, they identified several key influencers within the sales organization whose knowledge they needed to really understand what would motivate the sales reps. Would the sales reps in different areas react differently? As they learned more, they added more members to their RAP.

First, group your list of RAPs according to a simple A-B-C priority system, because some projects are always more important than others. Then, within each RAP, track the quality of your relationship with each of the names on the list, grading each along what I call the **Co-Elevation Continuum**.

Most of our relationships exist in one of five relationship states along this continuum. The most common, where most business relationships reside, is what I call the *coexist state*. In this state, people work together to get their jobs done but remain respectfully out of one another's way, even if they're assigned to the same team.

We typically acquiesce into the next state, the *collaborate state,* when we find we can't accomplish our jobs with the resources and responsibilities under our control. We come to this state out of necessity. We collaborate when we have to, but only for as long as we have to, before scurrying back to the default, the coexist state.

When collaboration becomes too challenging, we tend to fall into what I call the *resist state,* which manifests as tension and stress between us and a teammate or colleague. While in this state, we passively or consciously avoid authentic collaborative engagement—even when it would boost our chances of success.

When there is no personal trust or affinity, where attempts to collaborate lead to frustration, that's a relationship in the *resentment state*. In this frame of mind, we've pulled back from attempts at further developing a professional or personal relationship and make little more than surface attempts at collaboration. Think of a tortoise withdrawing into his shell.

The last of the five states, the *co-elevation state*, is the ultimate state, the holy grail of transformative relationships. It's the state we should strive toward in all of our relationships.

After you've identified the quality of each relationship along the continuum, assign them a simple number using the following scale:

−2 Resentment state
−1 Resist state
 0 Coexist state
+1 Collaboration state
+2 Co-elevation state

Let's say you've assigned Bob in accounting a −2 (resentment state) because you've had a particularly strained relationship with him in the past. Now that you recognize he's a team member in one of your A-priority projects, you'll want to be proactive about addressing whatever issues you have with him so you can raise the quality of your relationship upward on the continuum, toward the co-elevation state.

Put the RAP to Work

The RAP gives you focus, so you know which critical relationships on priority projects need your special and urgent attention. Having multiple RAPs gives you a managerial shortcut to prioritizing the co-elevating relationships you most want to focus on and the shared objectives that need the most attention.

Tracking these numbers allows you to keep an eye on your progress with each individual, while also tracking your aggregate progress. When you add up all the scores on the RAP, the closer you get to an average score of +2, the better you're doing. A number of months after Sandy started using the RAP system to co-elevate with multiple teams, she was pleased to discover that her overall RAP average score had climbed from –1 to +1.6. It gave her clear evidence that her hard work was paying off.

Measuring relationships this way doesn't make those relationships transactional. To me, it helps to single them out for how important they are. Occasionally I will share my score with a person I am co-elevating with in order to discuss what I hope we can accomplish together. I might approach Niles, for example, and tell him, "I have been keeping track of what I feel are the most critical relationships to this project, and I'm embarrassed to say I haven't really engaged you and your peers in the group as much as I should have. That's my bad. I would love to work together with you to remedy that."

> By embracing co-elevation, we are breaking down historic silos at Hudson's Bay. Co-elevation supports a culture of accountability—where we not only own our work but take initiative across the organization for work that will propel us forward. We can only succeed if we work as a team, committed to each other and committed to delivering for our customers. No boundaries, no silos.
>
> HELENA FOULKES, CEO, Hudson's Bay Company

TRANSFORMATIVE TEAMS, TRANSFORMATIVE RESULTS

Following the success of the incentive program, Sandy was promoted, and began a new project aimed at transforming human resources from a subordinate, functional role within the company to a key driver of business growth. This is a growing worldwide movement within the HR field, and Sandy has since become an expert and respected speaker on the subject.

Before Sandy and Jane embraced each other as *teammates*, they were pitted against each other, function versus division. Their industry, like most industries, is facing tremendous pressure to cut costs, as well-funded low-overhead fintech start-ups lure younger customers away from traditional banks. The entire banking industry is under siege. Every one of the four tech behemoths—Google, Apple, Amazon, and Facebook—have either introduced or threatened to introduce bank-like products that will squeeze the banking industry's profit margins even more.

In response to these threats, the leadership at Sandy and Jane's bank needed HR to control costs and the sales department to increase revenues. In essence, the bank was looking for transformative results by relying on incremental improvements. It was doomed to fail. There was no way for Sandy and Jane to create an effective new incentive program by glaring at each other from inside their respective silos. They first had to transform their personal relationship, and then they had to become co-elevating teammates with a shared mission.

Before Sandy's first meeting with Jane, I had suggested that Sandy be prepared to tell Jane, at the end of the meeting, what she was grateful for. Sandy bristled at the idea. "It will take some time before I can get there," she said, citing all the resentment that had built up between the two of them. So instead I asked Sandy to simply write down her feelings of gratitude after the meeting and share them with me, if not with Jane herself. Much to Sandy's surprise, a week later, as she sat down to write, she found quite a bit to be grateful for. Here is what she wrote:

I am grateful for Jane's help this past week recruiting some key sales people to our small working group that I would not have otherwise had access to.

While I am knowledgeable about designing comprehensive bonus programs, I am grateful that Jane brings the sales experience I don't have.

I'm grateful that Jane is willing to make time during her hectic days and evenings to get this right.

I was really grateful the other day when Jane heard me out on a way we could structure the bonus program that wasn't completely a departure from company protocol.

You know what, I really am extremely grateful that Jane is working with me in partnership, as I am making real progress when I was getting nowhere a couple weeks ago.

Sandy ended up sharing this note with Jane the next time they met, and sent a polished, appropriate version of it to the head of HR and the head of sales—Jane's boss. The relationship between the two improved so dramatically that neither one could quite believe it. Sandy, having accepted Jane as a member of her team, was able to trust her and count on her in ways that had been unimaginable just weeks earlier.

It's an amazing story—but not that unusual. And all of it is available to you once you ask, "Who's my team?"

OLD WORK RULE: Your team is limited to those who report to you or report to your manager.

NEW WORK RULE: Your *team* is made up of everyone—inside and outside the company—important to achieving your project or mission.

OLD WORK RULE: Professional relationships happen organically over time and develop without purposeful effort.

NEW WORK RULE: Professional relationships must be proactively and authentically developed with the people on our *teams*. This is the new competency of collaboration and productivity. It is critical to getting things done, more quickly.

rule two

ACCEPT THAT IT'S *ALL* ON YOU

We want to go after problems that no one else has solved, and create things no one else has ever figured out. To do that, we need people who don't make excuses, who take the lead in innovating and lead without authority when it's necessary to get things done. Innovation leaders naturally learn by doing. That means they try things such as quick sketch prototypes, dry tests, or A/B tests. They learn from the tests that work, and especially from the tests that don't work. Every surprise is new learning for the innovator.

SCOTT COOK, chairman, Intuit

"At least five years."

That's how long an ER doc named Zina had been told she should wait for a promotion to management at her hospital in Los Angeles.

At age thirty-one, Zina felt she was ready to do bigger things in her medical career. She'd refined her skills on the front lines at a bustling downtown hospital and now wanted to more deeply impact policy and overall patient care.

"My real passion is that I want to help rethink hospital management, and not just at our hospital—I'm talking about in healthcare overall," she told me. "I want to make a real difference in how our profession treats patients." But her boss told her that because she was relatively new at that hospital, it would take at least five years before she'd be considered for a managerial role.

I was having brunch with Zina at WeHo Bistro, not far from where I live in Los Angeles. Zina is related to a friend and client of mine, and I was glad to meet and talk careers with her.

"Okay," I said to Zina. "So, let's talk about how to do this in three years, not five. And let's break down your mission into three steps. While you're helping the ER become a leader in patient care, let's move to make the entire hospital a leader in patient care, so your work will be respected enough to take that final step toward reengineering patient care in healthcare overall. Did I get it?"

Zina shook her head as if I'd suggested something crazy. "I've been asking around," she said. "Everyone tells me that five years or longer is typical. Getting into management faster just doesn't happen in healthcare."

I hear objections like this all the time: "Your ideas won't work in our industry," or "You don't know how we do things here." It's absolute nonsense. Always. The fact is that the organizations with the most hidebound, hierarchical cultures are in desperate need of transformational leadership within their ranks. And hospitals are a prime example—when they fail to adapt, they are extremely vulnerable to change, disruption, and competition. Rigid company hierarchies are loaded with inefficiencies, which makes them ripe for impact by anyone willing to lead without authority.

When we think and act like co-elevating leaders, our potential as leaders will get recognized—sooner rather than later. That's the fundamental message I want to get across in this chapter. No matter what your status is within an organization, the way to be a leader is to start leading. Right now. Do the job before you have the job. That choice is always entirely in your own hands. And the way to begin is by accepting that *it's all on you.*

SEIZE RESPONSIBILITY

After half an hour talking with Zina, I was confident she was ready to make a tremendous impact at the hospital. She exuded the confidence, eagerness, smarts, and energy it takes to be an exceptional leader. And she knew that she wanted to be a patient care advocate, a goal perfectly aligned with her hospital's stated mission. Zina felt that the ER *needed* better management. It had real problems that weren't being addressed, and she wanted to take them on. That would be her path to opportunity.

"If you could wave a magic wand," I asked Zina, "whose performance would you improve in your department? Who would make the biggest difference in the ER if they did a better job?"

Without hesitation, she picked out a head nurse named Devon. Among his many responsibilities, Devon was tasked with ordering medical supplies for the ER. But he didn't seem to be doing the job very well. Certain supplies frequently ran out, sending ER doctors and nurses scrambling to borrow gauze pads, exam gloves, or antiseptic wipes from other hospital bays.

I suggested that Zina consider ways to help Devon improve his performance in keeping the ER supplied. "If you could help end the supply shortage, it would probably impact patient care. It's a start," I said. "And it's a great way to exercise your leadership muscles."

But Zina shook her head at the idea of helping Devon. "That's not my job," she said, adding that Devon was an older man with a prickly personality who had worked at the hospital for twenty-five years. "I try to avoid Devon as much as possible," she said.

I reminded Zina that she'd just identified an area that was *right now* negatively impacting her team in the ER and hindering the staff's ability to serve patients. But Zina was adamant. Devon would not take kindly to anyone trying to help him, she said. There were senior physicians content to keep putting up with the supply problem. None of them had ever addressed the issue with Devon.

Zina and I had just met, and I didn't want to scare her off, but I had a tough message to deliver. So I lowered my voice and took on a more intimate tone. I wanted her to know that I cared about her, her challenges, and her future.

"Zina, the problem here isn't Devon," I said gently. "The problem is you."

I asked her to examine how her fear of talking to Devon meant she was letting down her patients, the ER, and the entire hospital. Zina had just told me that improving Devon's performance would help the ER. Now she was claiming she couldn't do anything about it because it wasn't her responsibility.

"You've taken an oath to 'do no harm,'" I reminded her. "Why would you keep this fix to yourself? You're like Ebenezer Scrooge hoarding his money."

Zina reacted forcefully, which I appreciated. "I have no idea how to make Devon better at his job. How do I go up to Devon and tell him how to fix the inventory problem when I don't even know how to fix it myself?" she asked. "And even if I did know how to fix it, he's not going to want to hear that from me. I know him. He'll get defensive. He always does when someone says something that touches his turf, even without criticism."

I listened as Zina listed all the reasons Devon needed to change, and why she couldn't help him, before telling her, "Frankly, I don't care about Devon. Let's focus on *you*! If you're going to wait for everyone else to change, you might as well put your career on hold and be resigned to underperforming for your patients."

I've heard it so many times before: "They won't listen to me anyway. It will never work." It's a common excuse for not stepping up to lead, especially when being a leader is not in your job description. But real leadership is not about telling others what to do. It's about inviting others, encouraging others, getting others excited about new possibilities.

True leadership doesn't presume to have the answers. In fact, the opposite is true. The best leaders start with an open mind and invite others to seek solutions with them. Truly great leadership is about genuinely caring about the other person's success as you mutually learn and grow. That's true of all successful leadership. But it's absolutely crucial to leading others when you have no positional authority.

"I'm not suggesting that you march into the ER and start dropping truth bombs on Devon about how he needs to better manage the inventory," I told Zina. "You need to start by asking good questions." Zina didn't need to know any of the answers to ER's supply problem in order to take the first step toward being a leader, I continued. She only needed to accept that it was up to her to start co-elevating with Devon to find a solution.

TAKE CHARGE OF YOUR KEY RELATIONSHIPS

Devon was probably well aware that he had a problem, I suggested to Zina. But it was also likely that he considered it his problem alone to fix—even if he didn't know how. Perhaps he'd been trying to solve the problem, but there were other factors at play. It was also safe to assume that Devon didn't feel comfortable asking anyone for help. Perhaps he was afraid of the risk to his reputation. We all do this at times—we're afraid to discuss the elephant in the room because we're not sure we can handle the consequences.

I could see that Zina had heard me. And I suspected that this was her first real awakening to her own agency in becoming a leader. She had clarified her first goal—to improve patient care in the ER. And she'd identified Devon as the first person she could enlist on her team to help her succeed in that goal. For the first time, she could see that reaching out to a co-worker represented an opportunity for her to grow as a leader.

Building such relationships represents a new competency in the new work world. It is absolutely critical in tackling transformational change. Relationships come in and out of our working lives so frequently today that we don't have the luxury of letting them form haphazardly. Instead, we must proactively and authentically develop them, keeping in mind the specific tasks we want to achieve in partnership with them.

My recommendation was that Zina get to know Devon, and let Devon get to know her. She should suspend her assumptions about him so she could find out what was important to him at work and in his personal life. When I am in this situation, I find the best way to start is to ask the other person's advice about something you would like to know more about.

"Learn more about his day, ask him about his responsibilities, even his personal interests," I suggested. "But keep your conversations positive and steer clear of workplace gossip. Offer him a compliment about his work, but only if it is authentic. If you find yourself heading down to the cafeteria, ask him if you can bring him a cup of coffee. The next time, ask if he would like to join you. Swing by his station more often, get to know him better. Better yet, invite Devon to lunch. Share a little about your weekend, about yourself. Tell him what drove you to become a doctor, or what you like about living in LA compared to New York City. Put yourself out there, make yourself a little vulnerable. Show him that you're approachable. Most of all, be interested in him. Be curious about his interests and his life. Your goal is to build a genuine rapport with him. Share ideas with him; eventually, you'll look for ways to improve, to rise, together. Enlist him on your *team*."

Great leaders know how important this is. Cheryl Bachelder, who as CEO of Popeyes led a tremendous turnaround at the company's restaurants, has stressed the importance of this kind of relationship-building. "How well do you know the people who work for you?" she asks in her book, *Dare to Serve*. "Do you know the three or four events in their life that have shaped who they are today?"[1] Leaders with those insights are able to understand their team members' motivations and desires, leading to better conversations and fewer misunderstandings.

I continued to throw ideas at Zina. "Does he like cooking? Yoga? He lives in LA, after all." I chuckled. "Reading, theater, sports? If you share enough about yourself with him," I told Zina, "he may start to open up about the challenges he's facing in his life."

Zina was skeptical. In her mind, Devon was a difficult person she preferred to avoid. Talking to him felt like walking on eggshells. And here I was suggesting she get to know him better.

"Do you really think he'll be open to having a relationship with me?" she asked.

"In my experience," I said, "most people are." Despite the organizational barriers of insecurity and of hierarchy, our hearts are crying out for closer, more trusting relationships at work. People are eager to get help in talking through and solving their problems, and in helping others solve their challenges, too. But that happens only in the context of a relationship built around trust and authentic care. When people don't feel connected, they don't lean in to collaborate. When people don't feel safe, they shut down.

In Devon's case, I was pretty sure that he wouldn't feel safe confiding in Zina until he and Zina had built a more trusting relationship than they currently had. "As you work more collaboratively with Devon," I told Zina, "as you help each other to grow and develop, one of the easy ways to encourage him is to celebrate your progress together. Point out what he's doing that you respect. Without being condescending, be excited for him about any wins that you see."

Zina nodded. That made sense to her. She was taking notes.

"After you've spent time getting to know each other and you've built some trust and the beginnings of a relationship, then you can naturally migrate to the next level, which is to start collaborating with him on how to make the ER better. Start by telling him what you're working on—how you want to become a better ER doc and a stronger leader, how you want to serve patients better and up the quality of care overall. Ask him if he has any ideas on how to do this. Throw out a few modest suggestions—you don't have to lead with his ordering supplies more effectively. Ask him for his opinions. Have a dialogue, a genuine back-and-forth conversation, where you're tossing out ideas, listening to his, asking for his feedback, giving him yours. That kind of collaboration should become the foundation of any relationship you build. Finding solutions together for your shared mission of a better ER can become one of the things you look forward to doing together. You want to constantly collaborate. That's one of the core principles of a co-elevating relationship. I guarantee there will be even better ideas that the two of you will stumble upon together once you start peeling back the layers of the onion.

"After you are comfortable tossing ideas around on how to improve the ER's function, you could ask him for specific feedback to help you grow and develop professionally. Tell him what you're having trouble with and ask his advice on how to solve it. One of the goals of co-elevating is to go higher, to create an openness between you, and an invitation to grow and develop together. He has years of experience; ask him how you could improve your work and the quality of your performance. And if you don't agree with what he says, just say, 'Thank you.' He's not doing your review—you just asked for his opinion. If he gives it to you, he is doing so out of a spirit of generosity. Tell him you are happy to return the favor anytime, if and when he wants.

"One way to segue from this into improving the inventory management system in the ER is to ask Devon if there is anything you can do to help him. Try to find a way to be of service to him in his job. By now, you should have permission to make an observation, in the spirit of being helpful, that inventory management seems like something that could benefit from attention. Ask him how it works. Tell him you would like to learn more about it. That maybe you could be of help to him with an extra set of hands. What I'm describing doesn't have to happen quickly. If he rebuffs you, go back to building a stronger relationship with him, getting to know him better. The goal is to keep at it. Remember, you want to be doing this work, developing these skills, for years."

That said, I told Zina that it might not work out with Devon. That is always a possibility with any relationship. The importance of taking that first step is that until you try, you really can't know if someone will make a good teammate. If Devon turns out to be unreceptive, I told her, she could shift her focus to other people, and another problem in the ER.

"I know I just threw a lot at you," I said. "But the process I just described—building a co-elevating relationship with Devon and perhaps with others in the same way—is how you start leading the transformation of the hospital today and perhaps go from waiting five years to being made a manager sooner."

Zina nodded, and replied, "I want to give this a try."

By the time brunch was over, Zina was ready to take the first step: to try to get to know Devon better, and ultimately establish a co-elevating relationship with him.

"Work at it," I told her, "and try it with others besides Devon as the opportunities arise. Start being a leader with those in the ER now, and I guarantee you'll make manager in no time."

And bottom line, I added, "Even if you don't get the management job in three years, at the very least you'll have learned a great deal. You'll have spent those years working to fulfill your mission to improve patient care."

KEEP PUSHING THE ENVELOPE

Zina and I stayed in touch over the subsequent months, and she gave me updates on her progress. She took to heart that it was her responsibility to reach out and build a relationship with Devon. In essence, she had already begun the co-elevating process, without Devon even being aware of it. To aid in her efforts, she also approached a highly respected older nurse, a motherly figure to many in the department, for some advice and coaching on how to work more closely with Devon. The older nurse was glad to share her insights about Devon, who to her had once been a youngster. Once she was convinced that Zina's intentions were genuine, she was generous in offering her advice.

Over time, Zina and Devon began to talk more often, first about work challenges, and eventually about themselves. Zina told Devon about her husband and their baby daughter, and Devon, whose children were grown, recalled memories of raising his own children. They often took their breaks together or had lunch together. As they grew closer, Devon saw himself as a bit of a mentor to Zina. They discussed the struggles their jobs presented. As the relationship deepened, they began to collaborate on solutions for making the ER run better.

Over time they volleyed ideas back and forth. It was Devon, often prompted by Zina's sometimes naive questions, who came up with many of the fixes for the ER's inventory supply problems. It wasn't long before supply shortages in the ER were a thing of the past.

In the process, Zina learned that there was much more behind the scenes at the hospital than she had ever imagined. Many of the solutions she and Devon devised required changes in procurement and accounting, areas well beyond Devon's control. Their conversations inspired Zina and Devon to develop co-elevating relationships with people in those departments. Zina felt embarrassed by how quick she'd been to blame Devon for all the ER's inventory problems.

I've never met Devon, but I've encountered hundreds of Devons over the years. He became open to solving the ER's problems because of Zina's decision to co-elevate with him. In Zina, he found someone who had good intentions about the future of the ER, and also had his best interests at heart. Zina had Devon's back. Devon took some of Zina's coaching and, Zina noticed, became less defensive and more open to others at the hospital. He also became more comfortable expressing his innate curiosity, because it was yielding results. "I don't know" became an expression of wonder instead of an admission of ignorance. And together they created a true co-elevating relationship.

Zina told me she believed that Devon just needed to be reengaged by someone he could trust. No boss assigned them the tasks they took on together—they just took the initiative and ran with it. Position and authority didn't come into play. As a doctor, Zina was higher up in the hospital's pecking order, but Devon, with his twenty-five years of tenure, had seniority. They worked together as teammates, focused on adding value to the mission of the ER and to each other.

Co-elevating teams like this have tremendous power. Those who have studied such relationships—from Hewlett and Packard to Lennon and McCartney—suggest that these kinds of dynamic relationships are deeply rooted in human nature. In their book *Team Genius*, *Forbes* publisher Rich Karlgaard and Michael S. Malone write, "Arguably, even more than language . . . it is this talent that singles out our species, an innate understanding that by partnering with another person, we can accomplish things we cannot do by ourselves."[2]

I think that might be part of the reason Hollywood buddy movies like *48 Hrs.*, *Thelma & Louise*, *Butch Cassidy and the Sundance Kid*, and *Men in Black* are so popular. We are naturally attracted to the story of two people thrown together under extreme circumstances who rise to the occasion, form a bond, and face their fears and challenges as partners. In a way, every buddy movie is essentially a tale of co-elevation. In buddy films, as in real life, change begins when one character reaches out to another, and then another, to spark transformation. *Les Misérables*, *Erin Brockovich*, *Selma*, *Norma Rae*, *Milk*, *Silkwood*—each tells the story of an individual who enlists the support of another person, and eventually an entire group, to take on a challenge and achieve far-reaching change. Zina and Devon changed the status quo. By co-elevating with employees throughout the hospital, they spread their passion for their cause: excellent patient care.

And Zina's five-year management track? When we last spoke, Zina reported that she had been promoted in just two years! She was also named to a number of hospital-wide improvement projects. By leading without authority, she'd earned a sterling reputation in the hospital as someone who showed initiative and vision, someone who could get things done. She'd made her leadership talents plain for everyone to see by generating results through co-elevation. And in doing so, she'd begun to shift the workplace culture of the entire ER.

Each of us has the ability, and the opportunity, to step up to be a leader in the new work world. I would argue that we have a responsibility to do so. For Zina, that change began the moment she put aside her excuses of "It's not my job" and "That person is too difficult." Each one of us has the ability to take a similar leap and begin to lead. Right now.

We have used co-elevation to raise up our leadership team and adopted it to discover innovative solutions to business problems with our broader, cross-functional, and multi-perspective organization. When you take responsibility for developing close co-elevating relationships with your teammates, you find you can overcome obstacles that previously seemed insurmountable. Co-elevation offers a practical approach to personal and professional development that provides a solid foundation for high-performing teams. Speaking plainly, it works.

JEFF BELL, CEO, LegalShield

RULE TWO: THE PRACTICES

If you're like others I coach or audiences I speak to, you may be thinking: "You just don't understand who I have to deal with," "You don't realize how much work I have," "You have no idea how difficult it is to get anything done here," or "What you're suggesting has nothing to do with my job."

If you're nodding along to any of these statements, then strap in. I'd like to help you discover how that kind of thinking is a self-sabotaging excuse that will lead you into mediocrity.

I empathize with the very real pressures, difficult bosses, or underperforming reports people face at work. I've used many of these same excuses myself. But I am not going to coddle you, because the stakes are too high. I know you're busy. I know about office politics; how some companies defer, delay, and dash initiative and new ways of doing things. I acknowledge that on the surface, it can feel easier and safer to just hunker down, do your job, stay in your lane, and let everyone else sink or swim on their own.

I get it. And none of it matters.

We've hit an inflection point where staying in our lanes is no longer an option. To have any shot at success today, with the relentless push to transform, innovate, and reinvent, we have to climb out of the bunker and reach out to the people who make up our teams. And when we find them, we have to do the work together: get to know them; work collaboratively; furnish genuine feedback; and offer guidance—and stay open to receiving all of the above from our teammates in return.

We can't wait for our team to find us.

If we see an opportunity, we need to dive in, just as Zina did. And if we discover that the other kids don't know how to share their toys or play nice, then it's on us to co-elevate with them, to step up and lead.

Redefining and broadening our relationships in these and countless other ways starts with recognizing that each of us is responsible for doing this ourselves. It's not the responsibility of our teammates, our boss, the company's leadership, or the organization's overall culture. Simply put, we create the reactions of those around us through our behaviors. Co-elevation doesn't require that both individuals agree. But in the end, you need to own the decision whether you want to have succesful relationships with your co-workers, bosses, clients, or partners.

This is the mindset one needs to shift from passivity, resentment, or resignation to the energetic determination to build a supportive team that achieves greatness.

Let me give you another example from my personal life. I've already mentioned that my younger foster son had difficulties adjusting when he came to live with us at age twelve. He'd already lived in fifteen homes and had been hurt so many times that his impulse was to push everyone away before they could reject him.

Would it have been appropriate or rational for me to expect my frightened, raging, emotionally brittle boy to meet me halfway? Of course not. I was the parent and my mission was to be a good dad and take care of him. It was on me to swallow my pain and frustration and do all the bending over backward. I had to head out to plead with his teachers on his behalf, and then go the extra mile to secure outside help. To do whatever it took.

On plenty of occasions, I still failed to be the calm adult in the relationship, but I always knew that it was all on me to pick myself up and try again. What was the alternative? To cross my arms and wait for him to "grow up"? Of course not.

If your mission is important, you can't wait, either.

I tell this story not because our teams are like children, but because I know that children are no different from any other human beings. All of us, no matter what age, respond positively to leadership and support that is offered with a steadfast commitment to the other person's success.

I'm also not ignoring the reality of difficult situations. I'm saying, instead, that if success matters to you, you're the only one who can overcome the obstacles in your way. Even when facing our most daunting problems, we have 100 percent of the power over how we choose to react.

Just as Zina recognized she could accomplish more at the hospital by enlisting Devon's help, we all can do more in our own worlds. To accomplish more, with full commitment and integrity, is one of the definitions of true leadership.

Imagine a group of executives joking over beers about how they cheated on their expense accounts. That would be an unconscionable violation of integrity. Yet when coaching executive teams, I consistently hear things that, in my opinion, are equally objectionable.

For example, you're sitting in a room and you have a point of view that you think would make a difference, but you withhold it out of fear that the comment may unsettle someone. Is it professional to just keep your mouth shut?

If you doubt the efficacy of a peer's direction, but you choose to be silent about the risk, is that acceptable or unacceptable behavior?

Is the act of speaking to others behind a colleague's back about their poor performance (without addressing it with them directly) high or low professional behavior?

If your goal is to act with integrity, to be a leader among your peers and in your organization, then the answer is no—failing to speak up is an abdication of your responsibility. Failing to take up the mantle of leadership and co-elevate with your teammates is a violation of professional integrity. My hope is that someday, failing to lead when leadership is needed will be no more acceptable than cheating on an expense account.

The truth is, you can build a relationship and work in partnership with anyone. Before I elaborate on how, I want to head off all the excuses that prevent us from co-elevating.

Avoid the Six Deadly Excuses

I've heard them all.

I know you're busy. I empathize. I know that some people challenge, test, and vex you. People are difficult sometimes. Heck, a lot of the time.

I'm not doubting the hurdles you're facing.

But none of our excuses matter. All these "reasons" are irrelevant to your real goal.

Believe me, I've faced challenges that made me want to back off and give up. I'm just saying that we each have to navigate our path to success, and often that path has serious hurdles and goes through some difficult people. It's also true that we might fail at times. That's inevitable. Author Seth Godin, the famous marketing guru I've personally learned so much from over the years, says that the expression "This might not work" can be found "at the heart of all important projects, of everything new and worth doing."[3] Uncertainty is where new value is created. Everything you want in life is on the other side of all your excuses for not trying.

No matter the situation, we have power over what and who frustrates us. But if we don't attempt to transform the critical relationships around us into co-elevating ones, we are choosing to be mediocre.

We've heard of the Seven Deadly Sins. Well, here are the Six Deadly Excuses we all must overcome in order to co-elevate and lead—with or without a title or official authority.

Excuse #1: Ignorance

Now that you are aware of the new work rules and that leading without authority is entirely your choice, ignorance is no longer an excuse.

Until Zina understood that she could be a leader in her job *now*, she thought it was perfectly okay to sit back and do nothing when supplies periodically ran out in the ER, putting patient care at risk. My message to Zina was that it was *her* responsibility to take on what was wrong at the hospital. She no longer had an excuse to avoid taking action.

And now neither do you!

Excuse #2: Laziness

Sometimes we fail to follow through and faithfully co-elevate with others because it feels like it's just too much work. The trouble is that in today's work world, despite the understandable difficulty we all have checking the boxes in our long to-do lists, you cannot afford to abdicate your responsibility to lead. If you hang back with a not-my-job attitude, you might wind up with not-a-job. If the mission is important, then you will do what you need to do to get the job done. Yes, co-elevation is hard work—but if you abdicate your role as a leader, you may find yourself forced to abdicate your business.

Most of us are satisfied with relationships based on simple coexistence. We're busy. Co-elevating relationships require extra time. It requires us to be proactive. And to be sure, many of us keep crazy schedules and are yanked in multiple directions. Even when we're feeling jammed, it's simple enough to fire off a quick email to set up a fifteen-minute phone call.

Co-elevation takes time, so you'll need to make room for it. That may mean delegating other responsibilities or reprioritizing your schedule. If you're managing a team or have people reporting to you, consider looking to them to do more. Some will leap at the opportunity to grow and advance their skills and responsibilities.

If you feel as if you can't catch a glimmer of light, try this: Ask those around you what you should stop doing or what you should do less of—in other words, ways you could save time. Their feedback may surprise you.

And if you don't have someone on your team who can take on extra responsibility, consider making this a co-elevation project. Co-elevate with someone who may, over time, be able to take on more responsibilities on the team. As you prepare and coach them, you'll also be freeing up time to nurture your co-elevating relationships with others.

Excuse #3: Deference

All too often I hear people resist taking the first step toward co-elevation in deference to the org chart. When a task crosses a boundary and requires the help of colleagues in other departments or involves advocating for a new initiative, I'll hear, "That's above my pay grade," or "It's not my call."

Someone once told me, "It's not my job to be my boss's coach." But if your boss happens to be the one person you need to engage with to make a difference—then, yes, when the occasion warrants, you might have to coach your boss. If you ever catch yourself being so deferential to the chain of command that you fail to speak your mind and hide the truth, you are not just letting yourself down, you're letting the whole company down. You're cheating your employer. It's no different than if you falsify your expense report. It's low-integrity, unprofessional behavior.

The truth is that often, people are waiting for you to dive in and become more involved.

Years ago, I founded a coaching software company called Pocketcoach. The head of product development at Pocketcoach, Mateo, had some brilliant ideas for taking the software in a new direction, but he held back because he felt he needed approval from our CEO and COO. As founder, I was prodding him to move ahead, telling him that if he believed so strongly in his ideas, he should put a presentation together and ask the COO for a meeting with me and the CEO.

But Mateo resisted. He was very young and had been bruised by prior rejections by the CEO and COO. He didn't want to risk going through that experience again. I remember how frustrated I felt when I heard his excuses for not trying. "They aren't your enemy," I assured him. "They're part of your team. Treat them that way. Recruit more people in the office to your point of view. Or put the presentation together and give it to me!"

So Mateo created a PowerPoint and got the meeting scheduled. It took only fifteen minutes for him to convince all of us that his idea was exactly the direction we needed to go in. And we changed some of our product offerings because of it. Ultimately, those offerings helped us sell the company.

All this happened because Mateo stopped abdicating leadership responsibility. Today he's running his own company and coaching his employees to lead without authority through co-elevation. He knows that collaborating without waiting for permission is the path to innovation, agility, and growth.

Excuse #4: Playing the Victim

One of the best things about accepting the mindset of leading without authority is that it can cure the disease of seeing yourself as a victim.

When people or events disappoint you, don't run away, resign yourself to the situation, or succumb to self-pity. Take the rational response and just treat accepting your disappointments the way you accept the forces of the market—as a reality to be dealt with.

In my work with large companies, I constantly hear complaints that co-workers are uncooperative or that the organization makes change too difficult or that the world is unfair. I hear more negative nicknames for rival internal departments than I do for competitors, which is where your organization's focus would be more suitably aimed.

I know this one excuse intimately because I lived it for years, telling myself and others stories that excused my failure to act in certain critical situations. I felt victimized after my CMO position was gutted at Starwood Hotels. I also blamed one of my early business partners for not pulling his weight. I used such stories whenever I had to justify why a project hadn't come together the way I'd envisioned, or why I needed to find a better partner, in business and in life.

On certain issues I was blind to the reality that I was just giving up, rather than doing the hard work of facing the conflict and owning my part in why a relationship wasn't working. I failed to fully develop the potential of the partnerships available to me. I fell short of my expectations in my professional and personal life.

It took me years to realize this was my own doing. Now I can see, with more compassion, how people can get so deeply invested in seeing themselves as victims that they make it impossible to succeed. When self-pity becomes a disease.

Instead of doing whatever it takes to get real results, lots of us play the victim card, clutching the victim mindset like a shield. How many of us never reach our highest aspirations because we pin the blame on circumstances or on someone or something else? How many of us suffer from déjà vu when a relationship or job ends in eerily the same fashion as a previous one?

Once we accept the idea that it's all on us, the excuse that we're the victim goes away. That understanding gives us total freedom to act, to build co-elevating relationships, and to lead without authority.

Excuse #5: Cowardice

Again, if a situation scares you, there's probably something in it calling you to grow.

Often we fail to choose co-elevation because we are too timid, too afraid of conflict, or too fearful we'll be rebuffed or rejected. That inhibition may be all in our head, but the fear of relationships is strong and ingrained. Most of us don't like to confront others—and I'm right there with you! Studies show that the pain of rejection is indistinguishable from physical pain.[4] But by experiencing what can be gained by leaning into that discomfort, it starts to get a little easier.

A few years ago, I was helping Kyle, a newly appointed CEO, guide his company through a significant turnaround and take the company public. Kyle had never held the top position before, and he found himself unsure of his ability to pull off the huge task that confronted him. His fear turned to anger, and he started shutting people down, even belittling them. Many felt they were being bullied.

The team under Kyle withdrew, fearful of speaking with him. They started to doubt their own abilities, and they began sending memos requesting his sign-off on the smallest of details. Kyle became overwhelmed with decisions, raising his stress levels even higher.

Results suffered, and the company's private equity investors began to fear they would miss their financial goals. Connie, the company's head of customer experience, realized that things would not get better unless someone on the team swallowed their fear of conflict and approached Kyle.

After a particularly contentious executive meeting, Connie told Kyle, "I really want us all to go higher together. You are the CEO, but you're also a member of this team who we need to support." She asked him to give her a day to meet with him to go over the current list of projects. Together they would agree on a course of action for each one, along with clear delivery dates.

Many on the team had complained that Kyle had too many balls in the air. But Connie was the first to turn that complaint into an action, for which she took responsibility. And Kyle was amenable to the suggestions Connie made because she framed the idea as one that was for the benefit of Kyle and the company.

Kyle surely knew his habit of lashing out wasn't the answer. He just needed those around him to help him through those moments, and to coach him to a better way of behaving, even though he didn't know how to ask for their help.

Connie, who'd pushed beyond her fear of conflict to offer a solution, had started the team on a road to recovery. Kyle continued to evolve as a leader, and the company blew by the expectations of the private equity group—not an easy feat.

"There's enough pressure from market forces we have to deal with so why let our own fear be yet another obstacle," Connie told me later. "Every turnaround needs co-elevation. I had to take a risk because I care deeply about our mission. And although he makes it tough, I had to take care of Kyle, too."

Excuse #6: Indulgence

Indulgence can take many forms. Caught in painful memories, we are often reluctant to relinquish our anger, our resentment, or our frustration. When a relationship is strained, we can simply be too prideful to give up being right, or too unwilling to view the conflict from another's perspective. But there is no place for clinging to resentment if it is holding you back from professional or personal success.

Resentment can be detrimental to our mental health and productivity. When we indulge resentments in the workplace, they just fester and get worse, undermining our careers in ways we might not even be aware of. Resentments between two parties can drag on for years in a downward spiral, costing both people incalculable numbers of lost opportunities for personal growth and professional success.

Remember—it's all on you! Break free from indulgent judgments, self-serving stories, and the pernicious habit of needing to be right or insisting that the other person reach out to you first. There's a professional, emotional, and physical cost to indulging feelings that keep us stuck and resentful. We give away our power, and fail to co-elevate, when we insist things have to go our way.

You Always Go First

If we want to succeed in a world where the pressure for constant change, innovation, and agility is massive and mounting, we have to seize the initiative. We have to change how we work with the people around us. If your goal is important enough, if it's a mission that you believe will make a difference on your team, in your department, or in your company, then you owe it to yourself and your organization to take the first step.

That's what Zina did with Devon. She had to take the initial step first. She had to make a conscious, concerted effort to change her relationship with Devon. As soon as Zina stopped avoiding Devon and began showing concern for both him and the performance of the ER, she and Devon were able to come together to form a productive co-elevating relationship that raised each of them higher, while addressing many of their department's problems.

But let me be clear. Co-elevation does not require consensus or two individuals having to agree. It only requires your taking *responsibility to decide* to be a co-elevator. Whether your relationship with your partners is going to succeed is up to *you,* and based on your actions.

In other words, you don't have to wait for others—you just have to get started.

When facing the challenges of raising my foster son, I didn't have the option to tell this rebellious child, "Hey, when you behave, I will be your father." The same is true at your job. If what you do matters enough to you, you have to give it your all. The excuses just don't matter. If your vision for the workplace, for your colleagues, for your career is important enough—and frankly, it needs to be—then act. Maybe you don't believe in your company's mission. But the bottom line is, if you are earning a paycheck, you owe it to the company you work for to give it your all. And you owe the same commitment to your colleagues. Even if the people you have to deal with are difficult or the relationship is fraught. In fact, more so.

Reconfiguring your relationships in this way begins with your recognition that it's your responsibility to develop and nurture them. Retired Navy SEAL commander Jocko Willink calls this mindset "extreme ownership."[5] To be a genuine leader, whatever your title, you have to be the person who owns that role for your team. This is the most important mindset shift that we need to go through in order to achieve great things. You can't wait for others. But you do have to start with others.

Always Ask, "What's My Part?"

We often don't realize it, but when we change how we behave and interact with someone, we change their response to us. Remember how Zina avoided Devon? She thought Devon was hopeless, that he was difficult to talk to and highly protective of his turf. But Zina changed all that by talking to Devon about himself and about the ER. Once she got to know Devon and the constraints he faced at the hospital, she recognized that the strained nature of their relationship was on her. In order to transform their relationship, she had to question what proved to be her unfounded judgments about Devon.

We all hold these kinds of assumptions and beliefs about the people in our lives. We make mistakes in judgment so naturally and reflexively that psychologists have a name for it—they call it fundamental attribution error. We observe someone's behavior and decide that's *who* that person is.[6] And the only way to overcome this fundamental error in thinking is to ask, "What's my part in that judgment?" and then take action to correct it.

When I encounter someone who I feel has brushed me off or isn't sharing their candid feedback with me, I try to look inward at my part in our relationship, instead of blaming the other person. Even after years of success, I often feel like an insecure kid from Latrobe, Pennsylvania. I developed a scrappy fighter persona as a coping mechanism. Self-reflection isn't my default instinct, and it wasn't my practice for years.

Today, I'll ask myself, "Why doesn't he feel safe to voice his opinion to me?" Then I'll reflect on how I can change my behavior.

When I encounter someone who, I think, lacks accountability or commitment, I will first question the clarity of my expectations and the effectiveness of my follow-up. Again, this wasn't an easily learned habit. It was actually born from my work with an astute coach in LA named Sean McFarland (I call him "Seano").

Seano's advice came out of his many years of work in addiction recovery. I met him when I was researching my previous book, and found his advice uncannily on target. At the core of Seano's treatment is the recognition that anyone trying to recover from an addiction must take full responsibility for her or his own recovery, with the help of others. You can't climb back from the depths of addiction while hanging on to a victim mindset.

I came to believe that we are all addicts, in one way or another. We are all deeply dependent or addicted to behaviors that don't serve us well. But we engage in them anyway. By borrowing some of the recovery concepts and practices I learned from Seano, I've helped many executives recover from their unhealthy dependencies on old work rules and the accompanying expectations at the core of so much workplace misery.

By getting clean with yourself, you have the power to improve any relationship in your life. Once you become aware of what you are doing—and this is an ongoing process—you'll be amazed to discover how often you've been giving up an important responsibility that has always been yours and yours alone.

Again, whenever you get derailed in a relationship with someone, you need to ask yourself, "What is my part in this?"

Ideally, you'd share the answer with your teammate. If that's impossible, then at a minimum, you want to fully understand the part you play in the direction the relationship is headed. If someone on your team is crucial to the success of the team or division, but you realize you've been resistant to co-elevating with them—perhaps because they set off your emotional triggers, or you don't like their personality—well, that's on you.

While the other person is only likely to co-elevate with you if you own your part authentically, you can often make a difference even without the other person changing their behavior.

In many instances, the relationship baggage and the personal styles are so seemingly at odds that it feels impossible to let go of whatever friction or resentment has built up.

Trust me, I know this one personally. There are a handful of people I'm in productive, co-elevating relationships with today that a few years ago, I'd have told you would never happen.

When I talk to people about the need to forgive someone, I often suggest they look at how they have reacted to and treated that person.

Usually it isn't the result of their best behavior or best selves.

You'd be surprised how receptive people will be, even those who have seemed antagonistic in the past, if you just say, "I'm sorry." If you reach out a hand.

Give Up Being Right

One of the chief obstacles to overcoming resentment is giving up your insistence on being right. It's a tough one. We're conditioned to defend our views and positions. But letting someone else be right is the act of prioritizing your mission over your "rightness."

I was once enlisted to help a large Texas-based oil conglomerate that needed its top executives in two particular divisions to work together more closely. Robin, who led all exploration and early production deals, and Chris, who led trading, shared many of the same customers, and it would enhance the customer experience if their efforts were better coordinated.

Unfortunately, Chris and Robin had never gotten along. In the few instances when they had to work together, they rarely saw eye-to-eye, and sometimes got into heated arguments at executive team meetings.

Chris was a successful executive who was making his numbers and thought his views on strategies and deals were always correct. Robin, who was also making her numbers, was sure she was always right. Neither tried to close the gap or see the other's perspective.

At first, I wasn't sure how I would get Chris and Robin to bridge their divide. I began by discussing how destructive silos can be to shareholder value; then I noticed someone was wearing a very sizable wedding ring (this was Texas, after all). I scanned all the ring fingers in the room and saw that everyone was married.

So, I stopped in midsentence and asked, "Does anyone here have a decent marriage?" At first, everyone looked puzzled, so I restated the question, and a few raised their hands, wondering what I was up to. Chris and Robin were among those with their hands up.

"Congratulations," I said. "You have all learned one of the greatest lessons in life: how to give up being right to get what you want." A few people chuckled, and I continued: "Men and women in strong marriages know what a well-timed 'yes, dear' or 'you're totally right' can do for the relationship and getting to a positive outcome."

I pointed out that in the bigger picture, where there are real disagreements, being more agreeable can make room for a healthier dialogue. Saying something like, "I may not be right about this, sweetheart," even when you don't exactly feel that way at the moment, communicates that you care more about the other person and your relationship than you do about being right. Drop the "sweetheart," and you have a solution for the workplace as well.

"Where else is it time for you to give up being right?" I asked. "Are there any relationships here in the room where it's time to give up being one hundred percent right?" I promised them I wouldn't actually make them say, "I may not be right about this, sweetheart."

As I spoke, I saw that I was getting lots of smiles and nodding heads. I even took the opportunity to joke about the relationship between Chris and Robin, which got both of them laughing at themselves.

Chris and Robin were both good people. And they were proud executives who trusted their judgment. They just needed to be reminded that indulging their resentment or feelings of irritation toward each other wasn't the path to being their best selves at work—or achieving better results for their organization.

I worked with the executives and their teams for several months. Whenever one or the other seemed to dig in their heels, I saw the other behaving markedly differently, in an attempt to preserve the peace and "give up being right."

It is uncanny how quickly and easily people can drop feeling resentful. And when the resentment is gone, you'll never hear anyone say they miss it. Why would they? Resentment leaves us blind and powerless; it's been compared to drinking poison and hoping the other person will die. When you take a moment to look at any situation that's making you resentful, you'll realize that whatever you're holding on to is mainly causing misery—for you.

> To realize our mission to empower every person and organization on the planet to achieve more, we want all employees to embrace a growth mindset and collaborate in new and innovative ways. We believe everyone at Microsoft can and should be a leader, so we developed a set of Leadership Principles—Create Clarity, Generate Energy, Deliver Success—to ensure that each employee feels empowered to bring their diverse perspectives and experiences to co-elevate toward our shared mission.
>
> KATHLEEN HOGAN, chief HR officer, Microsoft

A RAPID CLIMB, WHILE STAYING GROUNDED

After Zina was invited to join the hospital management team, I continued coaching her, through texts and phone calls. As the years passed and her confidence grew, she grew impatient at times, wanting to change things faster. That's natural, of course, when you are enjoying success and the mission is something as important as patient safety. But I thought I noticed Zina losing touch with her sense of humility.

She seemed to expect other doctors, nurses, and administrators to listen to her ideas on changing the system and jump to act on them, because she believed she saw things they could not. She began to indulge her impatience and dispensed with the need to build trusting relationships and enlist others in the shared mission.

At times, when she shared with me her frustration that others were not following as quickly as she'd like, I had to remind her to remain humble, to first develop her relationships in the hospital. When she indulged her impatience and her pride, she was in danger of shedding the superpower that had gotten her this far.

"Have you spent time building a relationship with the others in the ER?" I'd ask. "Have you found out how you can be of service to each of them? Are you engaging with and listening to their ideas in a collaborative way? Are you asking them for ways you can improve your performance?"

I would remind her to find fifteen or twenty minutes, a few times each week, to invite anyone who was frustrating her to have a cup of coffee. Remember, I told her, it was still up to her to initiate these relationships.

Before she had a title and management responsibilities, Zina had an easier time remembering that it was all on her to build such relationships. Despite being a busy ER doctor, she had established close relationships with nurses, doctors, and administrators throughout the hospital. With each new teammate, she had focused on getting to know them first, before enlisting them in the broader mission of improving the hospital and overall patient care.

Reminded of what had led to her rapid climb to management, Zina was soon back on track. She was attending conferences where the future of technology-enabled healthcare was being explored and helping to expand her co-elevating team beyond the walls of the hospital itself. Today, Zina is on her way to having an impact on extending human longevity, which was the reason she chose medicine as a profession in the first place.

OLD WORK RULE: Leadership is something bestowed upon you by the company or organization. It comes with the authority associated with your job title.

NEW WORK RULE: Leadership is *everyone's* responsibility. You must help lead your team, regardless of your job title or level of authority.

OLD WORK RULE: To advance in your career, you must do what's expected of you according to your job description.

NEW WORK RULE: To advance in your career, you should do whatever it takes to create value for your team and your organization, even if it's not expected and even if it goes beyond your job description.

rule three

EARN PERMISSION TO LEAD·

> Earning permission to lead speaks to what I believe to be a truth about leadership: the model of the strong, driven, smart, charismatic leader who provides direction, sets goals, and ensures everyone complies is a thing of the past. People do not want to be told. They want to be part of something. A new type of leadership is needed that is human, authentic, purposeful, and is about creating the right environment for others to flourish. This type of leadership will create trust, unlock self-motivation, and is needed to unleash extraordinary performance.
>
> HUBERT JOLY, executive chairman, Best Buy

My tech start-up Pocketcoach was running out of cash. I wasn't about to fold because I believed wholeheartedly in the business—bringing peer-to-peer development to an online platform. But I was struggling. Having already invested many millions in the company, I was prepared to pump more of my personal wealth into realizing my mission. But I couldn't do this alone. I had already raised a great deal of money from so many people I knew and respected. I needed new investors, and fast.

A mutual friend from business school put me in touch with Ken, a prominent angel investor and a well-respected figure in the Los Angeles tech community. Everything I'd heard about Ken made him sound exceptional—his smarts, his savvy investments in tech start-ups, even his ownership of an iconic LA bar. Ken also had a reputation for being a deeply committed investor, which was what I wanted.

I met him for brunch at a café in Brentwood with my company's pitch deck in my back pocket.

Our conversation began on the subject of Pocketcoach, but I wanted Ken to understand my motivation for founding the company. I spoke about my childhood in Western Pennsylvania, steel country. I told him about my family and how we struggled at the edge of poverty whenever there were factory layoffs. My personal mission, expressed through Pocketcoach, was to help people change their behavior and realize their potential in a work world where coaching is largely absent. I also wanted the technology to scale Ferrazzi Greenlight offerings for businesses we hadn't yet reached.

We'd been talking for an hour when I caught myself in midsentence. I realized that I'd spent so much time talking about myself that I had discovered almost nothing more about Ken than I knew when I sat down.

The fact that the conversation was so one-sided is not that unusual in start-up fund-raising. The investor is auditioning you, not the other way around. And Ken, like many smart angel investors, is a master at drawing people out and getting to know what makes them tick.

But just talking about myself wasn't going to allow me to open a deeper interest in him for a more important relationship. And by talking about myself, I'd likely done little to earn Ken's permission to move toward anything more to me than a prospective investment in his portfolio.

So I switched direction in midstream. "Tell me about you," I said. "More important, what can I do to help you?" I'd heard that one of Ken's companies was developing a new blockchain technology platform, and I asked if there were any Fortune 500 CEOs he wanted me to introduce him to.

I think Ken was disarmed by my questions. He looked uncomfortable and demurred. So I tried another angle: I asked if any of the other companies in his portfolio could make use of my corporate relationships. Again, he politely declined, saying that most were not quite ready for the light of day.

That's when it struck me that Ken might be focused on other aspects of his life more than business. If he wasn't interested in my professional connections, perhaps I could be of service to him personally. "What does the next year really mean for you and your family?" I asked. "Personally. In your wildest dreams, how would you like to end the year?"

Ken took a long pause, weighing whether he should say what he was thinking. I primed the pump a bit by sharing my own situation: single for the first time in twenty years. "Boy," I said, "is that an adjustment."

For the next twenty minutes, Ken opened up about his painful and protracted marriage separation proceedings. They had dragged on for months, and Ken was worried his kids were caught in the middle between him and his ex. Also, he confided, he'd begun a new relationship that he was struggling to make sense of. All these issues were weighing on his mind. By speaking openly and authentically about my upbringing and even my personal life, I had laid the groundwork for Ken to speak to me with vulnerability about his own life.

As Ken unburdened himself, I asked if he was getting any professional support. He admitted he'd never seen a psychotherapist in his life. So I offered to connect him with Sean McFarland—Seano—who had now become my personal coach. I even offered to pay for Ken's first session.

"Seriously," I said. "That's how much I believe in this guy, and how much I truly want to help. I do this all the time for friends. I promise he will make a difference."

Ken just stared at me. I wondered if I had gone too far, but I pushed through that fear, and without hesitating, I grabbed my phone and sent an introductory text to both Seano and Ken.

When you reach out to others with this kind of bold generosity, some people are taken aback. They may feel suspicious, fearing that they will somehow be in your debt. Or they may feel too scared and vulnerable to admit to wanting help, as perhaps Ken did on the professional front earlier in our conversation. But I did the only thing you can do in such circumstances: I put my motivations clearly on the table and assured Ken how much the possibility of our relationship meant to me, even though we'd only just met. And I meant it—making a commitment to co-elevation means you make a commitment to being boldly of service.

"Ken, your reputation is extraordinary," I said. "I want you as an investor. But it would be an honor to one day count you as a friend, too. I think there is a lot we could do together." I thanked him for his generous insights and advice. "I really don't want to let this slip by as just another investor meeting," I said. "Establishing a friendship and professional collaboration of real mutual benefit would be awesome."

He said that he also felt touched by our conversation, and thanked me for my generous gesture and warm words. And yes, he did agree to invest that morning—even without having seen my pitch deck. But what started that morning was so much more than an investor relationship for me, and for him.

Following our meeting, Ken began sessions with Seano, and in subsequent months I saw him open up to a new path of personal growth. Over time, Ken and I have developed one of my most powerful co-elevating relationships. We have both done well as a result of our professional collaboration, but the best thing that's come of Ken's investment is our rich friendship.

When we invite people into our lives to play important roles in whatever mission we have, we have to be willing to give of ourselves. We have to give a lot—even more than we ever expect to receive in return. Leading without authority requires us to engage and enlist others in this way to earn the trust and faith necessary to lead.

Invariably, when the company faced challenges, Ken was one of my closest and most helpful confidants and advisors—and similarly, when one of his companies was hit with a serious setback, I was there for him, at a time when many others had pulled away.

Years later, Ken told me he'd never experienced an investor meeting like our first brunch—and hasn't since. Never had someone gotten so direct and personal so fast, and never had he seen such generosity from an almost total stranger.

Most people who come to Ken just want his money. Many also want his advice. I knew from my research that I wanted much more. I wanted to earn his permission to engage in a co-elevating relationship that would take us higher together. And to do that, I couldn't hold back.

I went big with Ken because he was an accomplished person with whom I felt a kinship. I wanted him on my *team*. I had to create real value for him, well beyond any return on investment in my company. I wanted him to passionately sign on as an investor, and to *feel* connected and engaged with me, personally and professionally.

POROSITY: OPENING UP TO CO-ELEVATION

To co-elevate with our teammates, we need to be adept at opening up ourselves to them, as well as working to open them to us and our mission. If we want someone to join our team, again, we need to do the work up front. And if and when it becomes a struggle, we must be the first to suspend any prejudgment or sense of ego and defensiveness. We need to keep offering until our teammates see the value in joining and reciprocating—in sharing our time, energy, resources, knowledge, and emotional commitment.

Opening up a teammate to this journey must be a deliberate effort, like the effort I made with Ken. We need our teammates to see the value in sharing their time, energy, resources, and knowledge with us. We need them to say yes to joining us on a shared journey.

This ability to enlist team members and sustain their commitment is perhaps the most widely *undervalued* competency among leaders attempting to achieve transformational change. Why? Because while the rate of change is growing exponentially, our openness to change and to each other is rare and not growing at all.

From my days at Deloitte to the present, I've seen attempts at organizational change fail because key individuals were not open to change. If individuals are not prepared to come to the table and participate in a change movement, no amount of spending on process, strategy, or technology will deliver the desired results. Change is about people, and if people are not open to change, there will be no change.

This single factor is so fundamentally important to the success of change initiatives that at FG, we've engineered a measurement for people's openness to change. We call it *porosity*. It is related to the quality of being porous. Liquids are absorbed into substances with porosity in the same way we want our invitations for bold change to be absorbed by our teams.

We use porosity at FG to measure each individual's ability to absorb new thinking and take on new behaviors. The more porosity we can inspire in others, the more likely they are to hear our message, join our mission, and dive into some breakthrough thinking. My conversation with Ken was about inspiring him to expand his porosity toward me and envision what engaging with me might offer him. Over time, our porosity to each other has expanded to the point that if one of us reaches out with an idea, the other is usually on board before we even hear the details.

Years ago, at a seminar offered by Landmark,[1] the personal development organization, I heard a great definition of a "meaningful conversation": You've had a meaningful conversation when you leave the other party feeling "touched, moved, and inspired." That simple phrase has always struck me as very true and powerful. For any important conversation with a potential team member or co-elevating partner, let those three powerful words—*touched, moved, inspired*—serve as a touchstone. We want them to see new possibilities, and they'll be predisposed to saying, "Heck yeah. Let's go!"

The formula for porosity and preparing others to co-elevate starts with what I call *serve* and *share*. These two complementary concepts are so important that they are dominant themes running through almost everything I write. Think of serve and share as two strands in a DNA double helix, with each strand supporting and reinforcing the other. To serve is to lead with generosity. To share is to open yourself up and build the bonds of true connection and commitment with others.

FIRST, BE OF SERVICE . . .

My success in building effective networks has always relied on generosity. It's my prime directive. In any situation, I'm always asking myself, "How can I be of service?" No matter who I build a connection with, I'm wondering, "What do I have to offer that would make their life better, easier, more joyful, productive, engaging, satisfying, or rewarding?" If the potential relationship is of particular importance to me, I prepare for a meeting by researching and assembling at least five "packets of generosity"—five ideas or approaches that I've thought about in advance that I believe might be useful to the person with whom I'm meeting. For my meeting with Ken, I came in prepared to open up my network to help him or any of his companies. I also knew he had children of college age, so I was prepared with advice and contacts related to internships. When it turned out that Ken's big issue was his marital separation and possible need for counseling, I was ready to book him a paid-for session with my personal coach. The point is that I didn't hold back. I came to that brunch loaded with double-barrel generosity.

Adam Grant, author of the bestseller *Give and Take: Why Helping Others Drives Our Success,* has spent years studying the benefits of being generous with our time and expertise. I first met him when he was a professor at the Wharton School. He reached out to me after reading *Never Eat Alone* and wanted to know more about the special role of generosity in networking, what I referred to as "giving without keeping score." We've since become friends and have shared and learned a great deal from each other. He quotes me in his book: "I'll sum up the key to success in one word: Generosity. If your interactions are ruled by generosity, your rewards will follow suit."[2]

Adam has found that the individuals he calls "givers" are those who give as a way of being, as a way of showing up in the world. They give others their time, energy, resources, and knowledge. They create more value for others than they ever hope to receive in return. Adam has developed a significant body of research proving that givers rank among the most successful, productive, and effective people in business. That's partly because givers are more adept than most people at requesting and accepting help and resources when they themselves need them.

"This is what I find most magnetic about successful givers," Adam writes. "They get to the top without cutting others down, finding ways of expanding the pie that benefit themselves and the people around them."[3]

If generosity is important to building your professional network, it is even more critical to cultivating a co-elevating team to drive real change. Co-elevation demands real effort, and likely compromise, sacrifice, and casting off comfortable old habits.

It's not enough to ask, "How does the shared mission benefit the other person?" Instead, we ask, "How will the other person's life be improved by joining us in this mission?" Think hard; what do *we* have to give above and beyond the call to enlist and engage this person we hope to make our teammate? I will provide a number of methods for doing this on the following pages.

When we ask another person, "How can I be of service to you?" with this intention to blow them away, we can create an arresting and powerful "wait a second, what's going on?" moment. That's a vital moment of expanded porosity. He or she is poised to be more open to us and to our message, even if only ever so slightly at the beginning. Your offer of service can leave them touched, moved, and inspired to open up in a way they may not have dreamed of a few seconds earlier. I guarantee that on the day Ken met me in Brentwood, the last thing he was thinking was, "I wonder if Keith can be of any service to me in my divorce." That's the head-turning power of offering to be of service, of giving with generosity and not keeping score.

. . . THEN SHARE YOURSELF

After serving has given you some modest permission to build a deeper relationship with the other person, you can begin the shift to opening up authentic sharing that will deepen the connection.

When you speak with someone in a way that is humble and vulnerable, you tap into each other's humanity and encourage the other person to open up and take more risks with you. You're no longer "Cody from Accounting" or "Alyssa from Legal." You're an individual, with feelings, experiences, and goals, someone to whom your teammate can relate. Also, when you share more about your connection to your goals and your dreams along with your struggles, your teammates are more likely to feel moved, touched, and inspired to share what matters to them.

Genuine conversation isn't rocket science, but it's an art that is too often overlooked. No matter how busy you are, taking time to talk to and genuinely connect with others on your team, or those you hope to make part of your team, is, I find, one of the most rewarding and productive activities you can undertake.

As you listen and learn more about the other person, constantly be thinking, "How can I be of service? How can I help them overcome their challenges? How can I elevate them? How can I help them to achieve their aspirations and dreams?" Think in terms of the shared mission. "How will enlisting and engaging this person help the mission and help them?"

That is what I was doing with Ken over brunch. As your teammate's porosity expands, you become better equipped to give more. And as they receive more from you, they feel more comfortable sharing more, which allows you to serve and share even more of yourself. It sparks a virtuous cycle; the relationship grows and your shared mission comes closer into view.

Opening porosity is the path to the mutual connection and trust I believe each of us longs for, at the office, where we spend so much of our time, as well as in our personal lives. It's through these real, human connections that we earn permission to lead our teams, achieve our goals, and elevate our teammates—and ourselves—in the process.

> Co-elevation describes many of the critical capabilities that are required to cultivate our "in service to" culture, which has been so critical to our success. As the pace of digital transformation accelerates, we have redesigned our operating model to reflect the realities of radical interdependence, leaning on agile, diverse teams that can break down organizational silos and drive business outcomes without the need for traditional authority and control of resources. Success in this new environment mandates a new level of vulnerability and authenticity, creating the foundation of trust necessary for radical transparency and 360-degree candor.
>
> CHARLES MEYERS, CEO, Equinix

CHOOSE TO CARE

There's an old adage: Nobody cares how much you know until they know how much you care. The bottom line is that to lead effectively, your teammates must feel that you care about them. "Frankly, my dear, I don't give a damn," however suave when uttered by Rhett Butler to Scarlett O'Hara, is not an attitude that's going to fly in building a co-elevating relationship with your colleagues.

You have to make the choice to care, and you have to let your teammates know it. You need to tell them. Better still, you need to tell them and *show* them. In whatever way you can, make sure they not only hear it, but *experience* it.

During my initial brunch with Ken, I did a lot of serving and sharing. But toward the end of our conversation, it still felt to me that something was off, that we weren't really on solid ground. It felt to me that what was missing was a straightforward expression of my commitment to our relationship. I couldn't leave that unstated between us.

"Ken," I said, "I am determined to find ways that I can be helpful and of service to you—professionally or personally. I don't believe in one-way relationships, even with investors."

Sometimes you just have to come out and say it, just like that: "How can I help you?" They need to know you're sincere, that your generosity is real, and that you truly want to be of help.

Certain expressions of caring are indelible. Decades later, I still feel choked up when I recall how Pat Loconto, Deloitte's former CEO, paid for the flowers at my father's funeral when I was just a young man still burdened by school debt. But a word of caution: Don't say you care if you don't yet feel it or believe it. People will smell your insincerity from a mile away.

Some people put taglines on their business cards like "the connector" or "giving forward." I've always advised against this, because I fear it strikes some as too self-promoting. I've seen it make eyes roll. For the record, I do personally care for and admire some of the folks who use these taglines, and I believe their sincerity. I just find it's better to show up and be a connector and a giver without announcing that that's who you are.

Why is caring so important? Because when your teammates and potential teammates know you care about them, it grants you incredible permission to start the real work of co-elevation: fostering deeper collaboration and mutual development. Co-elevating relationships require two-way *candid feedback*—frank discussions and debates over your goals, the team's mission, and each other's performance.

I can't emphasize enough the power we each have to grow personally and professionally when we grant another person permission to critique our work. Creativity and innovation are ignited by exchanging ideas and giving each other our honest views as to which of those ideas are sound and might actually work. To do this effectively with your team and in a co-elevating relationship necessitates caring and trust.

You can be purposeful and focused about how you express your sense of caring without being manipulative about it. If you truly understand and accept that it's all on you to build your team in the new work world, then that's a challenge you can pursue with sincerity and authenticity.

You may not actually *like* some of the people you need to co-elevate with. But that's okay, as long as you pay them respect and genuinely want to help them to grow in service of the mission. When you're in the process of identifying who's on your team, you're not going to like everyone you need to work with to get your job done or complete a project—that's to be expected. You may need to put aside or shed your preconceptions and judgments of those with whom you've had a rocky past.

Just be earnest in your desire to co-elevate with them. The key is that they understand you're aware of *them* and their needs—and that you want to help them grow and rise. Again, it's not just about what you want them to do for you or the organization. They need to feel that you care about what's in their best interests, and that you're transparent about balancing their needs with the needs of the organization. This leaves no room for selfish agendas. So many of us cling to a desire for more power, influence, direct reports, or bigger budgets as a measure of our success. If the person you are working with gets a whiff of that, there's not much of a chance they are going to want to co-elevate with you. The North Star is winning as a *team*, together, not your personal glory or advancing your own agenda.

Hierarchical leadership is often the natural world order—especially in the start-up world. Yet it's simply not feasible (or desirable) once real scale is reached. When I first heard of Ferrazzi's concept and implementation of co-elevation, it immediately resonated with me as a modern methodology for agile servant leadership—an approach I embrace, allowing leaders and teams to respond, support, and serve as needs change. To be clear, this takes a huge time investment, but it is required to meet the pressures of today's marketplace, and I have found it time very well spent.

DAN SPRINGER, CEO, DocuSign

RULE THREE: THE PRACTICES

Let me tell you a secret: As long as you undertake this journey from a genuine and authentic place, you can't get it wrong. As Adam Grant says, "It takes time for givers to build goodwill and trust, but eventually, they establish reputations and relationships that enhance their success."[4]

Serve, share, and care is a journey of curiosity, candor, vulnerability, and action marbled together, a journey that only *you* can lead. It's not a step-by-step process. You're constantly searching to find what really moves and inspires those you co-elevate with, to make them part of your team. You are constantly thinking about the things they truly want and need in their lives and careers that you can help them attain.

The best way to help you navigate this is for me to offer specific suggestions, and leave you to pick and choose among them in your quest to expand porosity in other people. Here are some of the most powerful ways I've found that you can be of service to your teammates and incorporate deeper sharing into your interactions with them. You won't have to use all these suggestions at once, and you will need to pick and choose the right ones for each situation, but I think you'll find them helpful.

Forget the Golden Rule

"Do unto others as you would have them do unto you." That's the Golden Rule I was taught at Methodist Sunday school. As an ethical code, it's pretty reliable. Before you do something, consider how you'd feel if it were done to you. For most of us, that helps keep us on the straight and narrow.

As a tool for change, though, the Golden Rule has some obvious limitations. What motivates *you* and makes *you* excited to dive in headfirst is not necessarily the same thing that motivates those you co-elevate with, your teammates.

Earning permission relies instead on what I call the Platinum

Rule: "Treat others the way they wish to be treated." It requires sincere curiosity, patient listening, and learning about the other person. It's much harder to do, and it's fitting that platinum is much rarer than gold. All the platinum ever mined could fit inside a two-car garage.[5]

Because it's easier, the Golden Rule can be something of a trap. It can make you think well of yourself when you're actually being a tone-deaf, presumptuous jerk. I've fallen into this trap plenty of times.

Early on after founding Ferrazzi Greenlight, I was working with Miles, the chief marketing officer for a large food retailer. I liked Miles a lot. He reminded me of myself at his age, and that's partly why I found myself getting increasingly frustrated with him. As our young firm worked to help the executive team transform the company's go-to-market strategy, I saw Miles as the one person among his peers who could really step up and precipitate that change.

Over drinks before an executive team dinner one night, I tried to give him a pep talk. I suggested his initiative would differentiate him from his peers, who had grown somewhat complacent in their roles. He had a promising future in the organization and would be around to see the strategies we were discussing fully executed, while others would have retired by then. I suggested he could even be a candidate for the CEO role eventually. So many of the other leaders didn't seem right for the succession opportunity. Yet over the next few months, as we worked together, I couldn't understand why Miles avoided a number of reasonable risks that could have significantly advanced the company's market share, and his career. Miles's CEO made his thirst for innovation clear; he felt it was not just important, but vital, in order for the company to keep ahead of Walmart and other much larger retailers moving into the food space. So I kept pushing Miles to challenge his and the executive team's conventional wisdom. I thought about my own days as a corporate CMO, and how I would have jumped at the amazing opportunities for accomplishment and advancement that Miles was ignoring.

Despite my frustration, my relationship with Miles had grown into a real friendship. I knew I had permission to push him harder, perhaps, than others. Yet Miles was like an obstinate puppy. No matter how hard I nudged him, he wouldn't budge.

I was still fairly new to coaching, so it took me a while to recognize that *I* was the one with the problem, not Miles. He just wasn't as ambitious or driven toward the top job in the way I had been at his age. He placed a great premium on the role he had as the company's CMO, and the security it provided. He had no desire to scale the heights of the company, gunning for the next big job. He was where he wanted to be. My presumptuous talk of how he could be CEO and manage his career better was deeply unsettling to him, to the point where he was avoiding my advice, even when it made good sense to him. It was an important early lesson I needed to learn.

I hadn't been listening to who Miles was and what *he* wanted. He just wanted to do his job the best he could and serve the business. That was something I could work with. But to do that, I needed to drop the self-promotional promise of Miles's ascent, because that was standing in the way of his being able to hear me. I needed to just focus on our shared mission and help him succeed, *on his terms,* as the best CMO he could be, for the sake of the long-term competitiveness of the company.

It was not that Miles lacked interest in realizing the professional potential I saw in him. I'd seen him stand up to and triumph over the juggernauts entering the marketplace, and lead a successful transformation within the executive team of product, merchandising, marketing, and distribution strategy. While other businesses in their category imploded, his company thrived by carving out a defendable and profitable position. Miles never did become president or CEO of the company. He was happy leading the new marketing and distribution strategy, and leading his peers to step up as well. He retired early to pursue what was most important to him: his passion for cycling and creating a wonderful home life with his new bride. My experience with Miles helped me recognize the importance of knowing the other person's unique value perception and finding ways our shared mission will fit it.

However, there will be times when a teammate's wishes don't align with the project at hand. Good professionals will often have perfectly viable but different views on addressing a given challenge. It's in situations like this that you'll be reminded why you've been making such an effort to build solid co-elevating relationships. When you both value your relationship and recognize that you are collaborating in service of the mission and each other, you are more willing to take the time to generate greatness out of your disagreements. There will always be disagreements, and sometimes the easiest solution is to acknowledge, upon reflection, that your idea should take a back seat and you should let someone else be the hero. Or, you can both agree openly to work hard to push beyond your opposing positions and find a better solution—but that takes deep commitment to the mission and each other.

When you're looking for ways to be of service to your team, be careful not to impose your own flavor of generosity on them without understanding their underlying desires and goals. Hear them for the powerful insights they are. You don't have to embrace their choices, preferences, goals, or aspirations as your own. But you do need to understand them.

It's a lesson that's worth its weight in platinum.

Seek the Blue Flame

You can earn permission to co-elevate with someone fairly quickly once you identify their emotional purpose, or what I call their "blue flame." We all have one. The blue flame is what gives our lives meaning; it's what we value most—our purpose, our passion, our calling. It's the aspiration that lives deep inside us. And when this blue flame is ignited within someone, it's what makes them bounce out of bed in the morning, eager to make a difference in the world.

You find someone's blue flame the way I did with Ken—by being genuinely curious. Ask them about themselves and see how they react. Above all, *listen*. In some of my work with indigenous spiritual healers, I've learned about the practice of having a "talking stick" for group dialogue. A ceremonial stick is passed from person to person, and only the holder of the stick is permitted to speak, ensuring that no one interrupts or tries to hijack the conversation. To force yourself to listen, try pretending you've handed your teammate the talking stick.

You will find that people show up in extraordinary ways when you help them fuel and fan their blue flames. If you can align their passion and your shared mission, increased porosity and openness to change is the natural result. People who were once closed off become open to hearing your message and engaging with you.

That's the suggestion I made to Rachel, divisional head of HR for one of the big telecom companies, when she complained to me about her boss, Malcolm, the CEO heir apparent. Despite her years of service to Malcolm, Rachel confided to me that she didn't think he felt the same loyalty to her as she did for him. He was likely to become CEO, and he had not signaled at all if she was in the running for a big job, like being the company's next global head of HR.

I asked Rachel if she knew what Malcolm's blue flame was. Was it pursuit of the top job? Was it money? Ego? Power? Impact? Without being an armchair shrink, I wondered if he was trying to prove something to someone else—perhaps even someone who was no longer alive, like a parent from whom he desperately sought approval. What was his blue flame, and why?

Rachel realized she had no idea, even though she'd worked for Malcolm for twenty years. But once she gave it some thought, she recognized that Malcom had always prided himself on being a visionary in their industry. Then she realized something else. In her twenty years working under Malcolm in the org chart, she had always been a very effective HR executive, but she had never once done anything to contribute to Malcolm's status as a visionary.

Almost immediately, Rachel began pulling together a proposal for a strategy document that forecast the company's future needs for human capital amid industry disruption and changing market forces. Working together on that project was exactly what Malcolm and Rachel's co-elevating relationship needed. It was the kind of document that Malcolm could bring to the board to be seen as a visionary leading a team of visionaries—a team that now included Rachel.

Each person's blue flame is as distinctive as their fingerprints: Find a way to be of service to someone by helping them turn it up and burn more brightly. It is one of the greatest investments you can make in someone—I promise.

Once you've identified a teammate's blue flame, you can continue to speak to that person's blue flame, directly or indirectly, in every conversation you have with them. Your role in a co-elevating relationship is to be responsible for your partner's growth and development just as a traditional manager would have for a direct report decades ago. You want to become the kind of person your partner will look back on years later and feel truly appreciative that you were there for them and supported them in their growth and their aspirations.

So when you find a teammate's blue flame, celebrate it and help them to nurture it. Share your own blue flame with them. Above all, let each of your teammates know that you care about their heart's passion. They will, as a matter of course, become more porous to you and your ideas, and together, you will have set the stage for a powerful co-elevating relationship.

Promise Joy in Your Partnership

To put it bluntly, many people feel that a lot of what they do at work is downright drudgery. They feel regularly disengaged, disconnected, and discouraged by their jobs. Maybe you're among them. Gallup, the polling and consulting organization, has been tracking workplace engagement levels for almost twenty years, and reported in 2018 that worker engagement had hit an all-time high—of just 34 percent.[6] In other words, two-thirds of us are just getting by at work each day, emotionally and intellectually disengaged from what we're doing.

That's why the promise of joy in your working partnership with your colleagues is an incredible way to be of service. Never underestimate how much it might mean to someone if you can offer them a renewed sense of purpose, possibility, vitality, excitement, or fun in their work.

For some people, just being invited to work with you as you lead without authority on a special project will brighten their day and make them feel engaged and connected. If you do your job in opening porosity with them, you can even build your brand around having cool things to work on with a great co-elevating group that really cares about the team and the mission.

Most people, when they interview for a job, feel a rush of possibility, a flicker of excitement about what they can do and accomplish in their new role. Years later—or sometimes within just months—the reality of the job turns out to be nothing like what they imagined. We have to be the ones who bring that sense of possibility back to those who work with and around us.

Studies show that about half of all employees say their work lacks real meaning or significance.[7] People don't feel their work matters, which in turn leaves them feeling alienated and disengaged. That should be a serious practical concern at all levels of management, because the same studies suggest that employees who derive meaning from their work are more than three times as likely to stay with their current employers than those who don't.

But the concern shouldn't be limited to managers interested in retention. This sad reality should be *everyone's* concern. We need to make a difference and become the change that we long to see. It really is a choice.

Finding meaning in our work is an important human need, more important than happiness, in many respects. There is a difference between a happy life and a meaningful life. Many people can be happy just by satisfying their own needs and desires. To lead a *meaningful* life, however, you need to do things for others, often by setting aside your own desires and sometimes even your own short-term happiness.

That's what's at stake when you lead without authority—the feeling of true fulfillment you will experience when you offer teammates a path toward finding and achieving something meaningful. Because co-elevation is based on relationships and not paint-by-numbers hierarchy, it has the potential to inject those feelings of meaning and significance that are lacking in so many workplaces today. And you can make it all fun again.

When in France, Speak French

While it may be less true today than it was a number of years ago, as an American, you'll definitely have a better time in a foreign country if you try to speak the local language.

In our stressed, "what's in it for me?" business world, pragmatism and transactional thinking are the expected language. A strongly felt point of view isn't enough to get someone to engage with you and your goals. Passion works best when it's backed by hard facts.

I first met Devin Wenig, former CEO of eBay, back when he was with Reuters and I was coaching his executive team through a big merger. At the time, John Reid-Dodick, then Reuters's chief HR officer, told me that what first gave him and Devin confidence in FG's methods had little to do with my rhetoric. Instead they'd been impressed by the articles I'd published in *Harvard Business Review* and elsewhere, with their well-developed arguments, backed by research data.

Devin and John believed deeply in the need for this kind of work with their team, but they were both also savvy, formally trained lawyers who expect their beliefs to be borne out by data. Our empirical research had demonstrated that candor, connectedness, vulnerability, and peer accountability all had measurable impacts on team performance and shareholder value. The articles had spoken to them in their language.

This was a case where well-grounded research and data opened up porosity at the early stages of the relationship—enough to then be followed with authenticity and generosity. So while some CEOs may certainly appreciate the personal and emotional growth they would expect to experience with co-elevation, it is ultimately the promise of measurable benefits that attracts their attention early on. We all need to be approached with clear and reinforced logic first, the language most of us in business are comfortable speaking, not just the promise of deeper relationships.

Tell Your Story

Empathy is the bridge to get you from where you are today to a stronger relationship, one ready for co-elevation. And the key to accessing that bridge? Vulnerability.

Most people don't believe me when I tell them that I'm naturally an introvert who has learned to be an extrovert. I do a lot of things with determination and purpose that true extroverts do naturally and with ease.

When I want to connect with people, whether it's on a stage or in a one-on-one conversation, I have learned to share my struggles, challenges, and failings with them. The good news is that I have plenty of them. I can talk about my blue-collar upbringing and the insecurity I felt going to elite schools with rich kids who had everything. I talk about my challenges with my foster sons as we've struggled to find our way together. I even open up about my difficulties with being newly single. I'm open about my shortcomings in past jobs, and the leadership skills I continue to work to improve today. These are all the things that I once hid for fear that I would be judged for my weaknesses.

I do this so everyone knows that I am on the same humble journey they are on. That's how we earn the trust of others: by demonstrating authenticity and expressing our own desire for our shared success. This sort of candid conversation, which can initially make some feel uncomfortable, quickly leads to barriers falling. The mask slips when we share our own deeply personal stories; it is a sure path to creating empathy and greater porosity.

I do all this purposefully, with forethought and intent. That is not to say that I'm inauthentic or manipulative. I merely recognize that vulnerability serves as an important access point in our personal and business relationships. There's nothing fake or contrived about being purposeful in establishing and strengthening relationships this way. It's an acknowledgment that deeper relationship-building is too important to be left to chance.

I wasn't always this way. When I started my career, I often felt deeply insecure (I still do at times). Upon meeting someone, I would brag, drop names, and scramble to establish credibility as quickly as possible. I hid my weaknesses. Today, however, it would feel false for me to stand on a dais telling others how to take on the uncertainties of transformative change without also acknowledging my own flaws and shortcomings. We have to climb down from whatever artfully constructed pedestals we use to prop up our insecurity. We have to step out from behind whatever walls and barriers "protect" us and join our teammates arm in arm in this shared, messy journey.

Author Brené Brown defines vulnerability as a mix of uncertainty, risk, and emotional exposure. A research professor at the University of Houston Graduate College of Social Work, Brown has studied the disempowering effects of shame for many years and has developed a theory on shame resilience. In her bestselling book *Daring Greatly: How the Courage to Be Vulnerable Transforms the Way We Live, Love, Parent, and Lead*, she writes, "We're hungry for people who have the courage to say, 'I need help' or 'I own that mistake,' or 'I'm not willing to define success simply by my title or income any longer.'"[8]

The point is not to be vulnerable for the sake of vulnerability, but for the sake of establishing authentic connection and trust with another person. Just as you have to be the first to do the work toward co-elevating, you also have to be the one to go first in establishing a connection with another person if you are interested in creating a relationship with them. You often need to be the first one to open up, to share your struggles, your professional and personal challenges, and your journey in a frank, candid, warts-and-all way. Sometimes, though, I mess up and hold myself back. I might be concerned that an executive from another culture might not appreciate my openness or might negatively judge me and my company. But holding back never works. Inevitably, in these cases, I see how my words land with the people listening to me in a much weaker way than I had hoped. Every time I've done this, I've always ended up regretting my choice to not be myself.

Years ago, people could try to build a relationship with a colleague by walking into their office and casually chatting them up, looking at the pictures on their wall or desk for shared experiences to bond over. "Oh, you play golf? I get out on the course every weekend!" As much as small talk pains me personally, there's still a place for these conversations. In my conversation with Ken, for example, we discovered a shared love for the Burning Man festival in Nevada's Black Rock Desert. We shared some laughs as we recalled our experiences there, which was fun, but not really important. With co-elevation, an exchange of this kind is just a door to take us beyond the superficial to discover passions or pursuits that are truly meaningful.

To find a shared passion, try asking about one of these four categories: family, occupation, recreation, or dreams. (The initials spell out "FORD," which makes them easier to remember.) Ask anyone some curious questions in these four areas, and you will see their blue flame burn brightly in one or another. Many people are not even fully or consciously aware of their blue flames, and that may be part of the value you bring to the relationship—someone who is curious and patient enough to help them identify their passion and align their life in that direction.

Finding some shared passion is not necessary in order to connect with others. We just have to share our own passions, what is most meaningful to us. In such moments, we get to truly reveal ourselves and show up in a way that invites our teammates to also show up. To inspire empathy and build connections, be prepared to go a mile deep into something that makes you who you are, gives you goose bumps, or chokes you up, instead of going a mile wide hoping to find some superficial point of commonality.

Really Check In

Many of our clients at FG have built and sustained deeper personal relationships with an exercise we call the Personal/Professional Check-In. It's a practice that encourages each team member to disclose what's of greatest importance in their lives *right now*. The idea is to try to avoid the polite chitchat and go straight to a deeper understanding of what's weighing on each team member's mind.

We first introduced this concept while coaching high-level executive teams to accelerate their empathy and commitment, and today people frequently tell me they use it religiously with everyone in their workplace. I do it myself in small ways in almost every interaction. In doing so, I try to open myself up, share what is on my mind, and invite others to do the same. It can be done in person, on a phone call, or over a video chat. I might call and say, "Hi, Joe, Keith Ferrazzi. How's rainy London today? How was your weekend? Yesterday was Father's Day here, and I have to say, it was the best Father's Day I've ever had. It was the first time that both of my foster sons warmly acknowledged the occasion. I was moved—it meant a lot to me. Anyway, I can't wait to really catch up. So, how are you? What's going on in your life?"

To make this kind of Personal/Professional Check-In, all it takes is your willingness to go first, and to share what's happening in your life—personally and professionally. Then ask what's going on in theirs, and listen to what they have to say.

Make this practice a habit with members of your team, and watch the magic happen, as prejudgments burn off like fog in the morning sun. I like to tell the story of Nancy and Jim, two executives I worked with. Nancy ran product development at a legacy manufacturer, while Jim ran sales at the company. The two were at perpetual loggerheads. Jim was a sarcastic guy who was very territorial. He excluded Nancy and her team from all but the most mundane aspects of sales. Nancy was afraid of conflict, and while she came across as very pleasant on the surface, she complained bitterly behind Jim's back that her team was constantly being dismissed and overruled.

God forbid Jim might allow them to suggest, even once, a better approach on how to go to market with the products they had developed.

Before their executive team's next quarterly dinner, Nancy got the CEO's approval to conduct a personal and professional check-in with everyone who would be attending the dinner. To Nancy's surprise, Jim genuinely leaned into the exercise. He revealed to his fellow executives that his wife, who had been his high school sweetheart, had been battling cancer for the past several years. He admitted that he'd been struggling under the strain, and he apologized to everyone for the times he'd been impatient or short with them. He told them he'd begun to consider early retirement so he could devote more time to caring for his wife.

Upon hearing Jim's story, Nancy felt profound *empathy* for Jim for the first time. She realized he was under intense emotional pressure at home—the kind of pressure she knew she herself would be ill-equipped to deal with—on top of the extraordinary pressure he was under at work. Almost instantly, she became more porous to a closer relationship with him.

A week later, Nancy invited Jim to lunch. She wasn't sure if he'd accept—it was the first time she had reached out to him—but he did, without hesitation. Over lunch, she told Jim she wanted to be more supportive of him in his situation. She proposed a way for sales and product development to work together that would relieve Jim of some of the time-consuming data-analytics duties he was responsible for that she knew he didn't enjoy.

In the past, Jim might have balked at giving up a part of his turf. Instead, he was open to her offer, and thanked Nancy for her generosity. Nancy then asked if there was anything she could do to help Jim at home, such as making introductions to some respected specialists she knew at a local teaching hospital. Nancy's cousin happened to be a prominent physician there, and Nancy offered to introduce Jim to him. "Nancy, I would be very grateful," Jim said. "*Thank you.*"

Jim's wife made a full recovery. Jim remained at the company, and his relationship with Nancy was reborn.

Today, whenever Nancy's team sends questions to the sales team—the kinds of questions Jim never had time to respond to before—he answers thoughtfully and promptly. Jim and Nancy even began to partner on new initiatives.

And their new relationship began because Nancy suggested a personal and professional check-in. Knowing Jim's situation, she was more willing to forgive his past conduct and lead with generosity, looking for ways to help him out, to serve him, which in turn opened more porosity in him. Creating a closer relationship together not only eliminated the biggest source of Nancy's frustration at work, it also smoothed the way for them to partner on numerous projects. And when their efforts helped them to exceed their revenue targets, the whole company benefited.

Help Them Be Part of Something Bigger

Remember, the mantra of every great co-elevating team is "Committed to the mission *and* to each other." It is a powerful formula, because it responds to two fundamental human needs—to belong, and to be part of something bigger than oneself.

Alienation is a disease of modern times, and we will inevitably find alienated individuals on our teams. The opposite of porous is "impervious," and every workplace has people who are closed and seemingly unreachable. The challenge is to awaken in them the desire to belong, that unshakable need to be part of a tribe that is ingrained deep in our DNA. It is what Alfred Adler, one of the founders of individual psychology, called "community feeling," and it is essential for our mental health.

I was coaching an executive team at a major chemicals company when the topic at dinner turned personal. The team members began sharing their current and past struggles, and they were doing it with exceptional candor and vulnerability. Then an executive named Doug suddenly announced, "I'm not going to share anything with you about my personal life. I don't think it's appropriate."

The conversation around the table came to an uncomfortable

halt. After a brief pause, it resumed, but with much less intimacy. It was a shame; the team had come a long way in just a few months. In past gatherings, the stress among the group had been palpable, but at this dinner, it was clear they had bonded more closely as a team. I could see the joy and caring in their interactions, and their results had been ramping up.

After the dinner, I pulled Doug aside. I gently made the point that, of course, he could share what he wanted. But I had a bigger question for him: Did he want to be trusted by his peers? Did he want to be connected with them, to be a valued and trusted member of this newly emerging, tightly connected team? And if so, what was his strategy to get there?

Everyone has a right to reveal themselves or hold back from revealing themselves to their associates, as they choose. But I was sincerely curious what Doug was trying to signal by judging our exercise as inappropriate.

Asking these kinds of questions—*without judgment or criticism*—can be extraordinarily powerful with people who are resistant to opening themselves up, who stand outside the team, looking in. What is their endgame; what is their goal? I like to inquire how they feel about their current projects and team members. I like to ask what they like, or don't like, about the dynamics of some of the projects they're working on. Is there a team they enjoyed working on in the past? Once I know what's missing for them from their current work situation, I can look for ways to include that missing factor in the future. Those who frequently alienate others are often carrying a wound of some sort that makes human interaction difficult for them. They deserve compassion, because it's a sad way to go through life.

What I saw in Doug's reaction was his fear and reluctance to step outside his personal boundaries. When I asked him after the dinner why he'd said what he did, he didn't share much, beyond reiterating that his personal life was just that—personal. I assured him that I respected his choice not to share.

But in our next meeting, I noticed Doug opening up to his peers a little more than he had previously. He offered to lend one of his support staff to another team member who was struggling with a deadline, while expressing admiration for her admission that she needed help, a rarity at this company. When the conversation turned more personal, Doug told the group rather casually that he was excited about the weekend because his older son, whom he spoke to only rarely, was coming home from college. Few people had heard him express excitement about anything before.

What shifted for Doug? With just a simple nudge, in the form of an empathetic question on my part and his subsequent reflection, he realized he really did want to be a part of something bigger. An increasingly bonded team was emerging within the company, and Doug wanted to belong.

I find that even the most alienated individuals often just need some safe guidance to wade into the tribal waters, to release the insecure little kid on the outside looking in, afraid of stepping in for fear of being rejected.

I can't stress it enough: We are all hardwired for belonging. We all feel the need to be a valuable and contributing member of a tribe. We all still long for that connection. And even if our hunter-gatherer roots lie in our distant past, instinctively we realize that our modern-day survival depends on rediscovering community.

Keep the Gas Tank Full (A Cautionary Tale)

Earning permission is not a one-and-done kind of exercise. If one of your co-elevating relationships fades or starts to slip down the Co-Elevation Continuum toward the coexist or resist state, you have to assume it's on you to get it back.

If you want to be a leader on your team and in the world, there is no other way. The farther you travel together down the road to co-elevating, the more closely you have to watch to see if your relationship gas tank is low on fuel.

I've seen countless successful co-elevating relationships fall into the coexist state (or worse) when teammates fail to keep the tank full. Years of co-elevating and its accompanying personal growth between two people can vanish in no time when new stresses arise or new priorities disrupt their shared goals.

That is exactly what happened between Jennifer, the COO at a large regional freight-handling company, and Meg, the company's CFO. Meg had a prickly personality, and Jennifer's relationship with her had been strained in the past. But when the two were tasked with drafting a new strategic plan to present to their executive team, Jennifer spent months building a successful co-elevating relationship with Meg.

Their strategic plan was a hit, and they led a genuine co-creative effort to get there. But afterward, without that shared task to work on, Jennifer and Meg's relationship drifted. They began canceling their weekly one-on-ones, and eventually stopped scheduling them altogether. They also stopped taking the time to huddle together for prep sessions prior to larger team meetings.

One day Meg abruptly announced budget cuts as mandated by the parent company's CFO. The other executive team members were shocked to have such bad news sprung on them in that way. After the meeting, Jennifer asked Meg if she could walk with her back to Meg's office. She suggested that in the future, Meg might consider giving the team a chance to solve the company's financial problems before they rose to the level that they had to be handled by draconian budget cuts handed down from their corporate parent. Meg did not take the suggestion well. She snapped that she was just complying with the orders within the chain of command. And, she retorted, if the other executives were unhappy about the reductions, they should have paid closer attention to delivering on their own revenue targets, or voluntarily reducing their budgets.

Jennifer was furious. And after working so closely with Meg just a few months earlier, she felt betrayed by how Meg had spoken to her. But as I pointed out to Jennifer when she called me, beside herself with anger, she shouldn't have been so surprised. Jennifer had stopped making those crucial efforts at serving and sharing with Meg, who she knew could be a difficult person. She had stopped their check-ins. She was no longer curious about Meg's blue flame. Meg's openness, her porosity, had closed, and her old attitudes toward Jennifer had resurfaced—all because Jennifer stopped doing the hard work that co-elevation requires. So when Meg received a directive to make budget cuts, she didn't bother to warn Jennifer. Nor did she even think to collaborate with Jennifer on alternatives. As a result, Jennifer, her team, and the whole organization suffered.

When Jennifer told me what had happened, I reminded her of the principle "Look for your part." When our teammates' behaviors slip, we have to ask ourselves, "What was our role in the matter? Why haven't we been more diligent tuning in to their needs?"

"How does blaming Meg help you and the mission of the team?" I asked. "Blame is irrelevant when it's our agenda, our mission that's being sacrificed. You didn't keep the fire stoked. That's on you."

> In a world where everyone has too much to do and some of the most important people you need on your team do not need to do what you say—even if they work for you—we need to engage and enlist others differently to achieve the mission at hand and earn the trust and faith to lead. Most employees are now on teams where none of their teammates are their direct reports. That's where the skills of leading without authority and co-elevation are most in demand.
>
> ERIC YUAN, CEO, Zoom Video

SHARED ORDEALS, FRIENDS FOREVER

In the years that followed our memorable brunch in Brentwood, Ken became a cherished friend. He was a tremendous help in assisting both me and Pocketcoach when the company ran into setbacks. As an investor and advisor, he was there for the company in our darkest moments. When we ran low on cash, he remained committed to us, invested more himself, and helped open some new funding vehicles. He became one of the few people I felt I could confide in when I was most shaken or down.

Then Ken ran into a streak of bad luck that threatened his own business. It was a tricky situation, and as he struggled to hold things together, many of his friends abandoned him. His hard times lasted for almost two years. I constantly checked in with him to see how he was holding up. Sometimes, when I was working out of town, I would fly back to Los Angeles just to have dinner with him and help him put his worries aside for an evening. When his invitation to an annual political event I knew he had always enjoyed in the past was "overlooked" (by one of those ex-friends running for president who no longer felt the need to associate with Ken), I brought him as my plus-one.

Ken remains one of my closest friends and confidants. We will be lifelong friends, because we have stuck with each other through thick and thin. Our shared ordeals only served to bring us closer. As each of us goes through life, we can make money (or lose money) with all kinds of business partners and associates. What's far more precious is having people in our lives who are willing to serve, share, and care.

SERVE: This involves leading with a generosity of spirit and action in service of the other person, and your shared mission or goals, which you plan for, evolve, and execute together.

SHARE: Vulnerably building connection and commitment between you and your team.

OLD WORK RULE: To convince your teammates to tackle a project or mission, you must make a passionate and persuasive case for it.

NEW WORK RULE: To invite your teammates to join your project or mission, you must first earn permission to lead through serving, sharing, and caring.

CREATE DEEPER, RICHER, MORE COLLABORATIVE PARTNERSHIPS

The job of leadership in the twenty-first century is to create an environment that's agile and collaborative, and this means cutting across teams and hierarchies. At Box, one of our core values is "Be an Owner." Any Boxer, regardless of their level or team, should feel enabled to lead without authority. It's all about creating teams that are execution-oriented, with a bias toward action. And most important, teams and individuals need to feel safe when they occasionally fail. We learn from these moments through candid yet supportive postmortems, and we embed these lessons into how we operate in the future.

AARON LEVIE, CEO and co-founder, Box

I was excited to learn in 2014 that Brian Cornell had been named CEO of Target. I had gotten to know Brian years earlier when he was president of Safeway. He helped our foundation, Greenlight Giving, start Big Task Weekend, which brought together corporate leaders, including Kaiser Permanente CEO Bernard Tyson and Beth Comstock, then with GE, to collaborate on improving public health and wellness.

Target had some serious problems when Brian took charge, but from what I'd seen Brian accomplish at Safeway, I knew the company was in great hands. Then, in 2016, Brian and his turnaround team hit some serious headwinds. Foot traffic and sales at Target stores either fell or were flat. Holiday season sales flopped. The company missed its Wall Street earnings targets for the year. Analysts sniped that Target was doomed, just another big box retailer ready to be crushed by the Amazon juggernaut.[1]

In February 2017, after Brian announced a $7 billion strategic plan to transform the company's competitive position, Target's stock suffered its largest single-day drop in company history.[2] Wall Street's verdict was that the company's planned investments in new Target-owned brand launches, store renovations, and online and home delivery improvements would never pay off. Target was throwing good money after bad.

It took just a little more than two years for Brian and his team to prove everyone wrong. By August 2019, Target's stock price had rebounded to an all-time high.[3] Revenues for fiscal year 2019 jumped more than 7 percent over 2017's results. Target's stock hit another new all-time high in December 2019. In the space of just twelve months, Target's stock value nearly doubled.[4]

One of the most notable features of Target's turnaround was the company's launch of more than *thirty* new in-house brands in those two and a half years. Target-owned brands have always been big drivers of Target profits, essential to the company's "cheap chic" identity. So Target set a goal of increasing sales of Target-owned brands by $10 billion, which required an avalanche of brand introductions unprecedented in retail industry history.[5]

Target's tried-and-true method for bringing a single new brand to market had often taken more than a year. Now David Hartman, head of Target's Brand Design Lab, and Stephen Lee, head of Target's intellectual property legal team, were challenged with the mission of designing and trademarking at least ten new brands every year, with the timeline for each brand just five months or less.

Failure was not an option. In 2016 retailers were going bankrupt and closing locations by the thousands in what the industry was calling a "retail apocalypse." It was the year of *The Purge* for brick-and-mortar stores. For Target to survive, Hartman's and Lee's teams would have to radically change their ways of collaborating in order to achieve outcomes no retailer had ever achieved before.

Disruption and the demands of transformation create impossible situations that demand impossible solutions. The teams at Target found their solution in a new form of deeper collaboration, what I call *co-elevating collaboration*. Driven by the company's audacious goals, Target's teamwork yielded transformative outcomes through fast and faithful execution of this simple formula:

Transformative Outcomes = Radical Inclusion + Bold Input + Agility

Let's break down each part of the equation.

Radical inclusion refers to a commitment to true diversity of voices and inputs in the collaboration process. It's all about unlocking and extracting uniquely powerful ideas and perspectives by embracing and engaging a much broader, wider team.

At Target, Hartman and Lee recognized that getting so many brands designed and legally vetted so fast would require including more people much sooner in the process. Hartman invited teams from marketing, operations, sourcing, and product design to contribute ideas very early on, instead of having the Brand Design Lab merely request comments on its work as it had before.

Due to the fast pace and outsize workload, most linear approval practices fell by the wayside. Previously, lawyers and paralegals from Lee's team had only been involved when asked for feedback, usually late in the process and in a check-the-box fashion. Now they were involved much earlier and more often, in a way that invited everyone in the room to offer guidance and take questions.

Radical inclusion drives breakthrough ideas and innovations throughout the organization by attracting employee viewpoints from the widest possible range of departments and areas of expertise. As Apple CEO Tim Cook says, "We believe you can only create a great product with a diverse team, and I'm talking about the large definition of diversity. One of the reasons Apple products work really great is that the people working on them are not only engineers and computer scientists, but artists and musicians."[6]

Bold input is the gift you receive when you solicit candid and courageous feedback from a radically inclusive team. When team members can engage openly in back-and-forth conversations, they debate what's working, what isn't, and what they should do more or less of. All ideas are brought together to be sifted, sorted, debated, and decided upon.

For the first time, members of Lee's legal team at Target regularly joined the branding brainstorming sessions that had previously been the exclusive domain of the Brand Design Lab. New concepts were shared in this open forum, and the viability and comparative strengths of various options were researched and debated right on the spot. It was like a shooting gallery for ideas, a far cry from Target's old method of working in silos, with teams exchanging polite emails and making formal presentations over the course of weeks or months.

Bold input of this kind naturally raised anxiety levels among some at the Brand Design Lab. "My teams got very nervous," Hartman recalls. There was a fear that the legal team's early input and participation might kill the design lab's ideas before they were fully developed. "For this kind of collaboration," he says, "you have to be able to swim in the deep water."

Look, bold input is not for the fainthearted. It calls on us to set aside our fears of being judged or rejected for our biggest, most daring ideas. Bold input leaves no room for conflict avoidance because everyone loses when team members withhold their thoughts out of anxiety or insecurity.

Agility is the method for putting radical inclusion and bold input into motion as a continuous iterative step function until we get it right. By breaking project cycles into shorter sprints and checking in more frequently, teams sharpen their focus on achieving short-term outcomes that drive the pace of change forward. This methodology, also commonly referred to as "scrum," arose in the 1990s among software developers who needed to discard traditional code-writing practices that were needlessly slow and cumbersome. When applied to other disciplines, agility makes it possible for transformative breakthroughs to emerge over weeks and months, rather than years, as ideas and design drive execution.

Target's dynamic, agile process centered on a weekly leadership meeting in which all would gather standing in a circle for a rapid-fire review of the branding work in progress. Hartman's and Lee's teams, along with team leaders from marketing, product design, and merchandising, would take note of where obstacles had arisen and coordinate solutions. Midweek working sessions often included someone from the legal department running real-time database searches of existing trademarked names and categories so that tweaks and adjustments to new brand designs could be done on the spot.

Iterating in this way reduces the risk of unnecessary pivots or going off track, which can cost weeks or months of lost productivity. Doing it right, however, requires integrating diverse points of view in an atmosphere of openness and candid feedback at every stage of design and execution.

By the second quarter of 2018, Target had achieved its strongest financial results in thirteen years.[7] Target's chief merchandising officer told Wall Street analysts in a November 2018 earnings call that the new aggressive brand-launch strategy was paying off.[8] In March 2019, *Fast Company* magazine ranked Target eleventh on its annual list of the world's fifty most innovative companies,[9] hailing Target for "incubating cult brands in-house."[10]

These are the kinds of results possible with co-elevating collaboration that draws on radical inclusion, bold input, and fast-moving iteration. Co-elevating collaboration creates room for authentic *co-creation*, with everyone gaining a more profound, holistic understanding of how to produce outsize results within the organization. Both Lee and Hartman say they now have a much deeper understanding of each other's disciplines than they did before.

All the teams involved—creative, legal, marketing, operations, sourcing, merchandising, product design—have emerged from the process stronger and with better insights into Target's entire value chain, which allows them to communicate faster, avoid simple misunderstandings, and respond to emergencies.

> Simply put, co-elevation is all about the team. When you have the right team members working as partners in a collaborative, inclusive, and agile work environment, you can expect great things. As we continue to evolve in this new fast-paced, digitally led world, we need to adopt a shift in mindset to reflect a more collaborative and agile work environment. Our ability to influence and lead without authority is a higher evolutionary capability that fosters meaningful partnerships based on shared goals and objectives . . . and, ultimately, creates a culture grounded in trust, authenticity, and respect.
>
> DICK JOHNSON, CEO, Foot Locker

WANTED: CO-ELEVATING CO-CREATION

Disruptive change demands this kind of authentic co-elevating co-creation. We all need to go higher together to find breakthrough solutions, whether on small individual projects or huge bet-the-shop initiatives like Target's. At all levels we need to land more innovative solutions in the market than ever before. We need to pivot faster in response to market changes and co-elevate throughout, so that every member of every team emerges stronger and better prepared for the next wave of threats lurking around the corner.

Perhaps I should be happy for the buzz these days about the need for work to be done by collaborative cross-functional teams. But for all the chatter, I seldom see breakthrough outcomes like those at Target.

Whenever I ask new clients about their collaborative practices, they almost always say the same thing: "We're a very collaborative team. We work well together." But it's a bit like asking my boy if he cleaned his room. On first glance, it looks tidy. But open the closets or peek under the bed, and it's a different story.

The Deloitte survey of HR professionals cited in the introduction showed that the vast majority don't know how cross-functional teams work or aren't able to provide them with coaching to improve their outcomes. In the face of industry disruption, the widespread failure of this most essential management competency is probably costing billions in lost productivity.

I recently sat with James, the CMO of one of the country's largest banking conglomerates, who told me how the consumer revolution in mobile banking is threatening to devour market share in many of the company's retail banking product lines. And yet his company's collaborative efforts to build a mobile banking product suite have floundered as leaders in the business wrestle over who should own it.

Should the leader be James, the CMO, who maintains customer data, tracks the latest consumer research, and was first to raise the issue with the executive team? Or should the head of retail banking run it, since her unit is the one most threatened? Should it be the chief digital officer, who was hired by the CEO to respond to digital disruption? What about the chief innovation officer, who was also recently brought on by the CEO to be an agent of internal disruption? Or the chief technology officer, who knows the technology architecture and controls the tech budget? Or maybe it should be the head of strategy, who had been sounding the alarm and has begun to consider a tech acquisition in the face of the team's failure?

Everyone at the bank agrees that they desperately need a robust mobile banking solution to remain relevant with a new generation of customers. But the lack of a co-elevating mindset and effective collaborative action has allowed the process to devolve into a stalemate over the fight for control. James admits the situation is deeply embarrassing. All those resources, all those brilliant people, and nothing meaningful brought to market. My stomach is in knots as I write this and recall how often I see similar situations in companies of all sizes.

In reality, established companies should be able to enjoy huge advantages over start-up challengers if they were to become first movers along with their already deep and loyal customer base. In 2016, when many assumed that Target was done for and circling the drain, Brian Cornell recognized that Target needed to invest $7 billion "to disrupt itself" and survive. But very few companies are able to get out of their own way and execute against that level of ambition. I've found that even the more progressive companies that have launched incubator hubs for innovative businesses are usually very reluctant to greenlight and fund the promising concepts they've been incubating.

In the 1990s, our team at Starwood Hotels, led by our very creative CEO, gave birth to many of the latest innovations in lodging. We started an unparalleled rewards program with no blackout dates. We designed the fluffy Heavenly Bed, with crisp white designer sheets replacing ugly industry-standard polyester comforters. We opened boutique, mid-luxury W Hotels with a trendy bar in every lobby. Our team was the vanguard of innovation for the industry.

Years after I left Starwood, I recall hearing about the founders of Airbnb making the rounds in search of start-up investors. At the time, I thought Airbnb's business model was interesting but not really viable on a mass scale. Why would people rent out rooms in their homes to total strangers? And who would want to stay in a private home and give up the predictability, privacy, and convenience of a branded hotel?

Today I wonder what would have happened if, back in the 1990s, almost a decade before Airbnb, a few kids from one of our San Fran properties had made the audacious suggestion that we include some very select private home rentals in the Starwood Preferred Guest program. The move would not have been that far of a stretch. Our inventory already included a collection of smaller independent luxury hotels in Europe.

Or perhaps such a wild idea would have come from the outside. What if our team had stepped out of our normal conversations and met with budding entrepreneurs outside the company, people we didn't ordinarily speak with? Could we have co-created some truly disruptive solutions with them? Could we have overcome our typical concerns about brand integrity and product consistency long enough to entertain such an outside-the-box concept?

As innovative and open as we were, I really doubt it.

But maybe, just maybe, if even one of us with influence at Starwood had been more open and eager, if we had sought different conversations back then, maybe Starwood could have launched our own version of what would become Airbnb.

Instead, look what our industry missed. Airbnb is one of the most valuable start-ups in Silicon Valley history. By the end of 2019, it was worth more than $30 billion, turning a profit and still growing.[11] Airbnb now takes in 20 percent of all revenue in the US lodging market.[12] It ranks second only to the world's largest hotel company, Marriott—which bought Starwood in 2016.[13]

RULE FOUR: THE PRACTICES

In the new work world, nimble, ambitious, and audacious are the essential elements of co-elevating co-creation. Whatever your title, whatever the size of the collaborative project, your job as a leader without authority is to bring more people in, help generate larger, more impactful ideas, and find ways to execute faster. It all starts with a process that fundamentally changes how you and your teammates think about, organize, and execute on collaboration.

Recontracting: The Essential First Step

Having coached hundreds of executive teams all over the world, I've seen how true co-elevating co-creation can't take hold until all the old habits of second-rate collaboration are laid on the table with their shortcomings exposed. This is vitally important, whether it's a two-person collaboration or a big cross-functional team effort. In one of the first meetings, if not in *the* first, take stock of all the historical routines and work-culture norms that had previously prevented you from generating outstanding results. Then collectively cast them out, like an exorcism.

That's one of the first steps in a process I call "recontracting."

The aim of recontracting is to ensure that bold input keeps flowing strongly through all the stages of iteration. Everyone comes together and agrees to engage in a new social contract of behaviors that support co-creation. Recontracting ensures that the promise of radical inclusivity gets delivered through bold inputs and iteration. It's easy, after all, to check the boxes for team diversity yet fail to get the value of inclusivity. The real challenge is sticking to processes and practices that will grant us full access to the team's wide diversity of voices and contributions.

Recontracting sets group expectations for how we will behave through the collaboration. It gets everyone on the same page. We ask ourselves, what up-front commitments to better practices are we willing to make together? Getting to breakthrough solutions is simplified if everyone agrees to a new collaborative code of conduct before the actual collaboration begins.

We begin the recontracting conversation by discussing our previous experiences with collaboration. This is a chance for the whole team to explore openly the shortcomings and disappointments they've experienced in the past as a way of understanding the behaviors and group dynamics the group wants to avoid going forward.

Your group can do this best through a small-group process called collaborative problem-solving (CPS). I describe how the process works in greater detail later, but for the purpose of recontracting, CPS begins by asking one big question: "What are the top ten issues most likely to hold back our collaboration, given our culture and past experiences?" Then the team is broken up into three-person groups to discuss the question for about thirty minutes. Each group records their responses on a flip chart and then returns to the larger group, where one person from each group gives their group report. The objective is to arrive at the most common collaboration-killers within your shared culture, and to give special recognition to what the group considers the top three. Everyone on the team is then asked to verbally promise they will avoid these behaviors. They also promise to point out with empathy and understanding whenever they observe themselves or other group members engaging in these behaviors. The key is to specifically agree, right up front, that you have permission to call out these behaviors without shame, merely in service of co-elevation.

Having officially exposed the undesirable collaboration behaviors, the group can then recontract for a new set of agreed-upon desirable behaviors. These behaviors vary with every group, so the rest of this chapter is devoted to discussing a number of the basics—such as a commitment to candor, methods for keeping emotions in check, and a preapproved process for breaking deadlocks.

Through recontracting, we each agree to do our best to drop the old collaborative behaviors and adopt these new ones. We all also agree to be called out when we fall short. Because we *will* fall short. We will screw up. Everyone will backslide into the old behaviors from time to time. Set that expectation from the very beginning and it will lighten up the inevitable incidents of backsliding, so everyone can just embrace the progress instead.

Recontracting can be repeated periodically over the weeks and months of the collaboration, as team members come and go. Each time, it can be done with a focus on new issues that might emerge during the collaboration. And while this chapter is mostly involved with group process, it's worth noting that recontracting conversations of this kind can be very valuable in setting standards of expected behavior in any one-on-one co-elevating relationship.

What makes the recontracting conversation so valuable is that we raise the bar for high performance while at the same time agreeing to accept each other's faults when we fall short. When we remind ourselves to have empathy for each other's old habits and rituals, it's so much easier to commit to supporting each other in forming new ones.

Confront Bad Collaboration

To begin the talk on past collaboration failures, you might want to give your team the bold-strokes outline of the Unholy Trinity of Bad Collaboration: Consensus, the BS of Buy-In, and what I call Bake-and-Ship.

Consensus is usually cited by grizzled business veterans as their primary fear, whenever I discuss collaboration. Many of them have been tortured by collaborative efforts that tried to placate every voice in the room and ended up producing useless, consensus-driven mush.

True co-creation is anything but consensus. In recontracting, the team must agree that they will stay true to the high standard of a truly transformative outcome, and that the final answers will meet whatever criteria the team is shooting for. A co-creating team must have a clear hurdle or bar that they set for themselves in order to make bold decisions, whether the entire group agrees or not. The goal of co-elevating co-creation is to find the most *powerful* choices, not the easiest ones, and certainly not the most popular ones.

The BS of Buy-In is that frequently insincere invitation to collaborate, aimed at gaining a group's acquiescence on decisions that have already been made. The proposition is something like everyone voicing their lunch preferences, only to find out later that the pizza order was already on its way. Buy-in isn't co-creation. It's sales—and who wants to be sold to?

The term "buy-in" is like nails on a chalkboard to me (I smile, as I know many readers don't even know what a chalkboard is). The leaders have committed to a solution, and they may put on a show of accepting feedback just so they can get consent for doing what they planned to do all along. In my experience, buy-in leaves people feeling flat, and less likely to put their hearts into execution of the plan. And when things start to go wrong, team members aren't likely to volunteer their feedback and proposed solutions because they've already gotten the message that no one really cares what they think.

Bake-and-Ship is my shorthand term for any process in which a small group goes as far as to interview and seek input from others first, but then crafts and presents a solution pretty much in finished form like Moses descending from Mount Sinai with the Ten Commandments. This is often the work of consultants or training programs rolled out from headquarters.

Some portion of every solution is pre-baked at the start. I find it very productive to begin a conversation with the humble assessment that maybe 30 percent of the solution at hand is already baked. The invitation to collaborate suggests we work together on the next 60 percent and then keep iterating and inviting others to contribute toward the final desired outcome.

But bake-and-ship skips all that messy interplay and the wonderful discussions essential to creating solutions that work. It's fast, efficient, and well controlled, but it sets up the team for uninspired solutions that are unlikely to resonate with your target audience, much less achieve transformational results. Bake-and-ship may have worked well enough for some companies in the past, but it's poorly suited to an age of rapid market change and disruption.

Here's an example of a typical bake-and-ship failure. Dave runs the Southwest region for a major insurance company based in the Midwest. His field sales managers were struggling against the entry of cheaper, mostly online, competitors. The solution from headquarters was to send everyone through a mandatory standardized half-day course aimed at making agents more responsive to their customers. The trainers at headquarters had taken many months to develop the course, and although they had consulted the company's field agents along the way, they only half-heartedly sought feedback on the finished product in advance of its official launch.

No surprise that the course was a flop with Dave's reps. The well-intentioned bake-and-ship solutions provided by headquarters proved to be a complete waste of time and resources. It was out of touch with the specific challenges the reps were experiencing in the market and offered little in the way of practical solutions. So, Dave decided to launch his own co-creative effort. He invited a handful of his best reps to an afternoon session to figure out how to increase their close rates by 20 percent. In that single afternoon (using the CPS framework), the small group produced a series of new selling points based on their deeper firsthand understanding of their clients' struggles and concerns.

Over the next three months, Dave's team cobbled together a set of customized solutions that met their clients' needs in ways that no monolithic online competitor could hope to match. These solutions created such breakthrough results that other sales regions came up with their own versions, copying the co-creative process that Dave's team had used.

Make Candor Compulsory

Before we start collaborating on a project, we must first be ruthlessly candid with ourselves: "Do we trust each other? Do we feel safe sharing our boldest, most critical ideas openly? Have we done the necessary, important work, to serve, share, and care with the broader team to make this collaboration possible?" These are foundational questions we must confront if we expect to maintain candor moving forward.

We will most likely have work to do around candor with our teammates before diving in with them. It's not necessary to be the official team leader in order to take a leading role in beginning the recontracting conversation. We just need to care enough about our teammates and team outcomes to take the plunge and advocate for more candid, engaged, and transparent collaborations.

Then, in the recontracting conversations, we must stress the importance of building a team culture of candor, on top of the permission we have created through serve, share, and care. The stakes are enormous, because nothing kills shareholder value in a company with more certainty than a culture of conflict avoidance. At most of the companies I work with, conflict avoidance is rampant and everyone knows it. Recontracting for co-creation is the perfect place to put a stop to the fear or avoidance of saying what we are thinking.

A culture of candor within your team unleashes everyone's contribution to the fullest and ensures bold inputs. This is why wildly successful entrepreneurs like Ray Dalio, founder of the hedge fund Bridgewater Associates, champion a workplace with a radically transparent culture.

"The key to our success has been to have a real idea meritocracy," Dalio writes in his book *Principles*. "To have a successful idea meritocracy, you have to do three things: 1. Put your honest thoughts out on the table. 2. Have thoughtful disagreements in which people are willing to shift their opinions as they learn. 3. Have agreed-upon ways of deciding if disagreements remain so that you can move beyond them without resentments. And to do this well, you need to be radically truthful and radically transparent, by which I mean you need to allow people to see and say almost anything."[14]

These are open discussions we need to have with those on our team if we are to build a culture based on candor. Even after recontracting, our fear of conflict is guaranteed to start creeping back into the collaborative dialogue. To maintain the candor on your team, try this from time to time: Ask everyone in the room to write down privately on a piece of paper how they rate the candor level in the room, on a scale of 0 to 5. Have someone collect the ballots and tally the results. If the room average is 3 or below, that is a great opening to discuss getting some group candor about the group's lack of candor! Something's not being addressed. What is it? Why are you not being forthright? Use the CPS process and put these questions on the table with the group. Or just ask everyone to write down confidentially what they think is not being addressed, and have these answers read out loud to the room. It's time to talk about what genuine candor looks like, and why everyone's avoiding it.

The key obstacle to candor on most teams and in most company cultures is a lack of *psychological safety*. People must feel *safe and secure in their positions* in order to risk speaking out and sharing their ideas and thoughts openly. Amy C. Edmondson, a Harvard Business School professor and leading researcher on the subject, says people who feel psychologically safe tend to be more innovative, learn more from their mistakes, and are motivated to improve their team or company.[15] They're more likely to offer ideas, admit mistakes, ask for help, and provide feedback.[16]

Studies of teamwork at Google showed that psychological safety is the one factor that all high-performing teams at the company had in common.[17] Google's researchers discovered that the safer team members felt with one another, the more likely they were to partner and to take on new roles. People on teams with higher psychological safety were also "less likely to leave Google, they're more likely to harness the power of diverse ideas from their teammates, they bring in more revenue, and they're rated as effective twice as often by executives."[18]

By the way, Dalio's firm is the exception that proves the rule. Bridgewater Associates is a relatively small company that is inundated with job applicants who are attracted to its extreme culture—so Bridgewater has the luxury of screening job applicants for their psychological makeup. Those who lack resiliency are not likely to be hired. The Bridgewater culture of radical transparency makes for a tough working environment. It works only because they hire suitably tough people who have candor in their DNA, who don't fear being challenged and don't shrink from challenging others.

Most organizations don't have that kind of ready-made culture of candor, so it's important to recontract for candor at the very start of every collaboration. However, we also need to set the collective expectation for the team to grow psychological safety through deepening relationships and serving, sharing, and caring, then, on the back of this relationship, keep that candor conversation alive.

Check Your Emotions

Once everyone's agreed to commit to being candid in their input and feedback, it's time to prepare for conversations, thoughts, and ideas that may hit some sensitive nerves. Passion is understandable—even encouraged—in collaboration, but it's smart for the team to discuss in advance how to work through any exchanges that grow overly heated.

Researchers studying what's known as "emotional contagion" have documented how we automatically synchronize our emotions with the facial expressions, voices, postures, movements, and behavioral cues of the people around us.[19] Raised voices of course are easy to recognize, but many people express their emotions more subtly—they cross their arms, scowl, turn down their mouths, or turn their bodies away from their teammates. In doing so, they risk arousing the same emotions in others and derailing the team's progress. One slip can begin a spiral.

The team might recontract from the start that each team member will take responsibility for stewarding the emotional climate in the room so that it nurtures innovation, creativity, and ingenuity. Another approach is to agree that anyone can interrupt an emotionally charged exchange that risks intimidating people or shutting down candor by calling out, "Red flag," at which point the team agrees to step back and observe their behavior.

It's taken me years to learn these skills. That's partly because my dad, for all his amazing qualities, had an explosive temper, which I adapted to by matching his loud voice with my own. Now when I find myself getting upset, I'll take a break, walk around the block, even ask to reschedule the meeting. I'll do anything to keep my emotions in check so I don't risk impeding my team's forward progress.

> Developing high-performance teams lies at the heart of all innovation and transformation. The new role of the team leader is to cultivate an environment of trust, empowerment, and constructive feedback that inspires everyone to pull together toward a common purpose. The art of co-elevation lies in guiding the process and knowing when to be flexible and when to be decisive as a leader. Priority setting is no longer a top-down affair. Rather, teams share joint responsibility and agile principles, working in short cycles and deciding together where and how they want to move forward.
>
> ROEL LOUWHOFF, COO, ING

Communicate Fast and Frequently

Co-elevating co-creation relies on a continuous stream of check-ins with critical constituents, proactively seeking additional thoughts and perspectives. A great way to solicit bolder and more frequent input of this kind is to develop the habit of firing off lots of quick emails with humble requests for feedback. I do it all the time with my team. Email allows your teammates to respond thoughtfully at their convenience, and I've often received great advice and breakthrough feedback just by asking.

If you're someone who clearly owns one area of the collaboration—

let's say you're the data expert, or you represent the marketing department—reaching out to peers and inviting their feedback sets a great example of candor and courage for the group. Try reaching out to the others to ask for their insights on how you could improve your contributions to the group.

Here's a template I often send to people who want my advice on how to elicit the most candid ideas and input. Tweak it to fit your style and voice:

Hi, Haley,

I want to make sure we are not missing anything, that we are getting the best and most provocative ideas that we can on [insert project or mission]. I'd really appreciate your absolutely candid feedback on how we can go even higher. If you were me, where would you go with this? What do you think we are missing? I'm serious, please don't hold back. Hit me with both barrels. If we don't get everything on the table, we all lose. Trust me, we will reconcile with all the other ideas and pick a bold path. So fire away. I really value your insights and perspective. Don't let us miss ANYTHING. If it's easier for you, feel free to call me.

Thanks!
Keith

If I don't hear back right away, I tend to wait a few days before following up with a gentle reminder: "Excited for your kick-butt feedback! Thanks in advance for your critical insights."

As leaders, our goals are to always stay positive and keep the conversation focused on ideas and processes for improvement. Avoid getting into debates or coming across as defensive. We want to keep the input flowing, and a negative response risks shutting off the tap.

If you're unclear about the meaning of their feedback, try to avoid responding defensively. It's okay to ask for clarification, but do it humbly. Use phrases like, "I'm not sure I understand." Try not to put the giver of the feedback on the defensive. Always express gratitude—even more than you feel is necessary—for their input, their suggestions, and their positive energy. Celebrate the people who are pushing the edges and taking risks with you. If you do get a wonderfully bold and surprising suggestion, send it around to everyone on the team; celebrate that person and thank them out in the open.

Cultivate Curiosity

When recontracting with your group, remind them what the Greek philosopher Zeno of Citium said, "We have two ears and one mouth, so we should listen twice as much as we speak." Leaning in and showing sincere curiosity in what others have to say is an important collaborative skill. If we only swim in our lane, earplugs affixed, we miss out on what could prove to be indispensable insights from others.

To achieve real transformation, we need collaboration that keeps expanding our vantage point, so we need to be vigilant and encourage more input. One useful tool for doing this during meetings is a process I call 5x5x5. One team member takes five minutes to explain a problem or an issue for which they are seeking input. For example, "I'm struggling with getting an associate engaged with our work here," or "I'm considering a fairly costly investment as a part of our solution." The issue should involve some degree of doubt, and the team member with the question should be truly curious to hear other points of view.

Over the next five minutes, other team members should ask questions so they can gain a deeper understanding of the problem, without suggesting solutions. Then, over the final five minutes, everyone takes turns offering very direct and candid feedback. The individual who receives the input thanks everyone for the gift of their insights and candor. As with any gift, it will be used as the recipient sees fit.

The 5x5x5 is a fast, refreshing collaborative exercise for any team. It functions like a power nap. And you can make it shorter and sweeter, or even longer, depending on the time you have and the questions being posed.

There is magic in exercises of this kind. Group cohesion forms, because the exercise shows we're all open to new possibilities. Research shows that good questions lead to more creative solutions and more effective decisions. Francesca Gino, a professor at Harvard Business School, says that asking good questions "allows leaders to gain more respect from their followers and inspires employees to develop more trusting and more-collaborative relationships with colleagues."[20]

Go Big or Go Home

The challenge facing all companies today is that real change does not come about through incremental improvements. It comes through what's commonly called 10x thinking. If the typical goal in your company is to achieve a 10 percent improvement in cycle time for new product development, ask yourself what it would take to achieve ten *times* that result instead. The magic of 10x thinking is that it forces us to think in such radically new ways that even if we end up achieving only a 2x or 3x improvement, that's still exponentially greater than what would have been gained incrementally.

Co-elevation is the perfect tool to begin tapping into those dreams and finding teammates and partners receptive to trying them out. You'll learn a lot. And, just maybe, you'll help your company go big before industry disruption threatens to send everyone home.

I work with some of the most admired companies in the world, and 10x thinking is extremely rare among them. It's just not where their daily focus is, and it's easy to understand why.

At Delta Air Lines, for example, the executive team is so operationally excellent that they are able to continually reduce costs and increase customer experience scores in reasonably predictable half-percentage-point increments. Those tiny percentages add up to big numbers in an industry with more than $800 billion in annual revenues.

As an exercise at an executive dinner one day, Gil West, Delta's COO, challenged himself and the team with a quick exercise in 10x thinking that we like to use in our coaching. He asked everyone to put aside their thoughts about half-point improvements. Instead, he wanted them to look at where they would focus their attention if their goal was to create *exponential* improvements for their passengers, employees, and shareholders.

In the first round of the exercise, the executives split off in pairs to discuss the subject for ten minutes. When each team returned, they shared with the group some of the ideas they had come up with that few of them had ever entertained before.

The range of ideas was astonishing. (I can't disclose any of them here, but as a Delta frequent flyer, I found one game-changing idea in particular extremely exciting.) The areas of focus ranged from developing new business models to rethinking traditional terminal design. One theme that kept emerging was reinventing the employee experience. Every one of those executives knew that if they were to take Delta to the next level of customer experience, they needed to think in 10x terms for Delta's thousands of associates.

What I love about this story is that this is one of the world's most respected executive teams. (Gil was among those who allowed Delta to pull away from bankruptcy to become 2019's top-ranked U.S. airline[21] and one of the most respected airlines in the world.) The depth of experience and talent among these executives is so profound that they likely have billions of dollars' worth of 10x ideas pent up inside them. And for the first time, they now have a process for exploring those possibilities and the opportunity to pursue some of their 10x imaginings.

The CPS: Using Small-Group Problem-Solving

To elicit the collective wisdom of any group, effective collaboration depends on receiving candid and bold input from *everyone*. That can be a challenge in larger groups, where only a few voices tend to dominate on particular issues, while other voices go unheard.

As described earlier, CPS, the collaborative problem-solving process, is a tool that should be used continually throughout collaboration. Here are more details on how it works.

First, put a question on the table. The question can be from one team member who needs advice in one specific area, or it could be a broader question meant to provoke bigger thinking and maybe some contrarian perspectives.

Here are some examples of what I think good questions sound like:

- What ideas have we killed in the past that we never should have walked away from?
- What could truly transform how we serve customers?
- If our company were to adopt some elements of the apps and other technologies that we all love in our own lives, how could our own customer experience be transformed?

Each question needs to be focused enough to fill the limited time available—between thirty and sixty minutes. Try to be simple and direct in forming the questions. Multipronged questions don't work as well, because there are too many elements to address in a relatively short period of time.

With the question on the table, send everyone into small groups of two or three to really grapple with the topic, and allow them whatever time is appropriate to the complexity of the question.

Psychological safety is at its greatest in a group of three, so in each of these small groups, the participants can work intensely and creatively with the greatest courage, risk-taking, and candor. There's less likelihood of a member holding back, and there is sufficient diversity of thinking. Everyone gets heard, and the small group is able to analyze and incorporate the individual thinking into a few coherent ideas. The design of CPS maximizes the benefits in large groups of radical inclusivity, while keeping the small-group benefits of psychological safety and social approval. It's another case of a solution that we developed at FG that accommodates basic human nature, what I call "working with gravity."

The small group meetings serve as a valuable analysis phase, so that only the most intriguing and useful results of their discussions are brought back to the larger group. At that point, another valuable psychological dynamic kicks in: The reports to the larger forum by each small group are more likely to be expressed with greater candor and courage than one would expect to hear going around the room in a big meeting. Why? Because the person assigned to report back to the larger group wants the social approval of the other two people in their smaller group. The small group's spokesperson doesn't want to look cowardly or let down the other members by failing to include the richness and candor of the opinions expressed in their discussion.

CPS has yielded some of the most exciting moments I've seen in collaborative meetings. Clever, out-of-the-box solutions emerge when small, safe groups take fresh looks at the issue. More introspective team members step up and give bold reports, with the support of their small group behind them. Above all, you avoid the big-group pitfall of everyone deferring to whoever has the most expertise or the biggest personality in the room. CPS reliably generates ideas that never would have had a chance to be aired and considered in a larger group discussion.

Celebrate Changing Your Mind

One great topic of conversation in recontracting is our common human frailty when it comes to changing our minds. We resist doing it—which is exactly why we must commit in advance to remaining open to this possibility all throughout the collaboration.

My favorite Ralph Waldo Emerson quote is, "A foolish consistency is the hobgoblin of little minds." In a collaborative environment, try embracing the idea that you may be wrong. If it turns out to be true, you've learned something, and that's a cause for celebration.

If you hear an idea or opinion you dislike, try to see it from the other person's point of view. Recognize that you are unlikely to be sure you are right until you are challenged by the robust input of others. When everyone recontracts to accept that even a great idea can be improved or perfected by bold input from others, it's much easier to keep an open mind.

The recontracting conversation is a great time for everyone to agree that changing one's mind or giving up turf in the interest of the greater mission is something that will always be celebrated. Throughout the collaboration, high-fives are in order the moment anyone climbs down from a previously set position or surrenders some ground to keep the ball moving forward. If you find that your own position has shifted and you're ready to concede a point, be sure to openly acknowledge the team members who helped you see the light.

We don't get 10x results by thinking we always have the answer—especially from the start. That's another reason I recommend approaching each new collaboration with the assumption that even with our best prior thinking, we are still at merely 30 percent of the final answer, and the rest has yet to be co-created. Again, be vocal that your hope is that the team can help get the solution to 60 percent, and then continue to work from there, fully aware that there are no 100 percent solutions in this fast-changing world. This is the exact opposite of seeking buy-in or bake-and-ship.

I once hired a young product developer for a digital start-up I'd founded, even though in his job interview he had offered completely off-base prescriptions for improving our online app. It was clear to me that he didn't understand our customers or our product strategy. But that didn't matter to me. What mattered was that he made me *think*.

His challenges to our approach were grossly misinformed. But they were bold and provoked me to doubt many of my own underlying assumptions. And he was right. We were ignoring a critical element of the customer experience. As I peppered him with questions about the logic of his recommendations, I began imagining new possibilities for our software, and soon the two of us were excitedly talking over each other.

This is why I always try to stay open to the broadest, boldest input, no matter how much I may disagree with it at first. It would have been easy to dismiss that young product developer as just another arrogant, ill-informed coder. Instead we hired him, and he went on to help lead the start-up's growth and eventual sale.

Bold and agile thinking of this kind is what separates winners from losers on your team and throughout the organization during times of disruptive change. Drew Houston, CEO of Dropbox, recalls the time another company suddenly launched a free product that competed directly with a Dropbox subscription offering that was at the center of the company's go-to-market strategy. Dropbox needed a new strategy fast. "Had we clung to being right or pushing forward on our plans," Drew told me, "we would have been toast."

Don't be toast.

Set Deadlock-Breaking Rules

It's vital during recontracting to have discussions about how the team will break impasses and deadlocks if and when they occur.

Temporary impasses of one kind or another are common in collaboration. Most can be dealt with by holding a CPS on the challenge or question at hand. When you have an impasse, everyone gets to shift their perspective back to the agreed-upon mission, and to each other.

In my experience, most impasses can be dealt with collaboratively. Everyone needs to acknowledge what's best for the mission. Those who are not on the "winning" side of the argument must let go of any resentment or attachment to being right and get back to working together.

Collaboration gets put to the test when a group becomes deadlocked on a complex project and no one has the authority to make the final decision. But a deadlock isn't necessarily a bad thing. When group members are holding on to mutually exclusive solutions to the problem, it's often a healthy sign that everyone is thinking big, aiming high, and unwilling to buckle in the name of consensus.

The ideal approach to a deadlock is for the team to come together with the aim of finding an even more breakthrough solution. Lay out all the key points of disagreement so that everyone has a clear view of them and can discuss them frankly without shutting anyone down.

That's real co-creation. Sometimes it requires yielding to another's viewpoint, if that's what takes the mission higher. Giving up your prior stance needs to be celebrated as much—if not more—than being on the winning side. What's needed in such circumstances is the up-front discussion that perhaps someone must give up turf for the project or mission at hand to really break through. We need leaders who recognize how vital that kind of acquiescence is. One of the major roles for any leader is to celebrate to the rafters the people who put service of the mission first.

In the case of very high-stakes decisions, this is very difficult to do. There are times when a stalled collaboration runs the risk of ending in the worst possible way: Under the extreme pressure of the situation, everyone falls into behind-the-scenes turf battles. In such cases, with limited resources and uncertain authority, our natural human tendency is to become hoarders, protecting what's ours and grabbing for more with both hands.

Again, the way to avoid this risk at the start is to recontract for something I call the Transformational Tribunal. Everyone agrees in advance that there may be times we need to seek tiebreakers, and we agree who will arbitrate the final decision in the event of a deadlock. Binding arbitration of this kind is common in professional contracts, and it belongs in every collaborative effort, even in the smallest groups of just two or three people.

For the tribunal, all the parties lay out their competing cases along with their candid arguments against the other cases in an open meeting before the agreed-upon authority or decision-making body. By then, everyone has agreed in advance that backchannel lobbying prior to the tribunal is unacceptable and that they will not do it. It's all in the open, and they have also agreed in advance to abide by the tribunal's decision.

Ideally the tribunal authority should be the lowest-ranking person around who has real decision-making power and agreed-upon objectivity. But in many instances, the CEO is the person needed to resolve big cross-disciplinary disputes. For transformational collaborative culture to take root and grow, the message must come from the top that seeking novel solutions, surrendering turf, and employing the new work rules are behaviors that will be commended and rewarded.

Land the Plane

In your recontracting conversations, the final points you want to cover are the rules for ensuring that measurable progress is made during each meeting. I always coach teams to "land the plane" so at the end of a meeting, everyone knows who in the group is walking away committed to acting and executing the next steps toward the final outcome. As a part of the up-front recontracted agreement, successes and the rate of progress need to be constantly and vigilantly monitored. That will give your most impatient team members the firm sense from the start that this collaboration is about real outcomes and will not be a waste of their time and energy.

Here are a few best practices for each meeting, which might be agreed upon by the facilitator (presumably you) from the start of the collaboration.

Set expectations at the opening meeting. If it's not yet time for a decision or if you're just getting broad and early input, it's important to acknowledge this much at the beginning of a meeting. Otherwise, some members of your team may feel the lack of a resolution at the meeting's end means the meeting was a waste of time. At the end of each meeting, I go out of my way to thank everyone for their input and promise to keep them posted on next steps.

Do a "yes, no, maybe" exercise at the close of the meeting. Let everyone know where you're at before you go your separate ways. Five minutes before the meeting wraps up, run down the key ideas that were discussed and offer your take on each one, in terms of yes, no, or maybe:

"Yes, we'll do it."

"No, it's not time for that."

"Maybe we should look into that more."

If you are the decision-maker in the room, you owe it to everyone to be transparent about the direction of team decisions. And if you're not the leader or decision-maker, you owe it to the group (in the spirit of mandatory candor) to ask the leader to run a "yes, no, maybe" exercise on the meeting's key points before the group disperses. This

way, everyone comes away from the meeting knowing what was decided and what the next steps are for each decision point. I usually
keep a running list of these points during the meeting, so that at the
end, when it is time to summarize the "yes, no, maybe" assessments,
everyone gets a sense of how the ball has moved forward. This transparency is candor in action.

These measures help keep up the momentum by focusing on the
shared mission, with action points in clear view. The risk always remains, however, that some people will feel the collaboration is not
worth their time. If you sense that a teammate is disengaged, reel
them back in by reminding them that you value their input and asking for their help and advice: "John, can you help me figure out what
we are going to do next on the sales incentives question? Or is that
better for a separate discussion?"

> The beauty of co-elevation is that it incorporates two concepts
> I've long relied on: "diversity of thought is the catalyst for ge-
> nius" and "people support what they help create." Co-elevation
> unleashes the full collaborative and co-creative power of high-
> performance teams to respond more nimbly and with more
> creativity than if they'd been locked in top-down structures.
> Real commitment to co-elevation principles gives rise to the
> kind of open, safe environment that energizes people to take
> on big challenges and do their best.
>
> KEITH KRACH, former chairman and CEO, DocuSign

SPREADING A REAL COLLABORATION CULTURE

In the spring of 2019, Stephen Lee and David Hartman were invited
onstage at an annual leadership conference attended by hundreds of
Target's top managers.

"You might not expect us to be onstage together—creative and
legal," Hartman told the audience. "But Stephen and I work together
on a pretty regular basis, which is a reflection of how fast the business

is accelerating." Together, Hartman and Lee pitched bold input, inclusiveness, and agility to other members of Target's senior leadership, because the method of organizing collaboration remains up to each of them; it is their choice how to co-elevate and co-create, and I agree with them that it can't be instituted from the top down. Which is why it was so important for Hartman and Lee to speak about their direct personal experiences.

Lee has taken the lessons he's learned from the branding work back to his own legal team, asking them to look for ways to make their process more fluid and better connected with the business concerns of the Target teams they work with.

"We tell our internal partners that we can be more efficient if we're plugged in earlier," he says. "If we adopt this kind of collaborative process, it can be less disruptive for them, because we won't be derailing things late in the game, but we have to assure them that it's safe, that 'We're not going to come in and start killing your ideas.'"

All the skills of co-elevating co-creation represent new and important employee competencies. In the new work world, our ability to master our area of expertise isn't worth much if we can't use it to collaborate at this kind of rapid pace. When I saw Brian Cornell at Target's annual management meeting, he told me, "Constant collaboration is at a new premium. It's no longer about hiring great talent. It's about hiring talent that will make the team great."

OLD WORK RULE: Collaboration is a fallback you resort to when you can't get the job done yourself and really need other people's cooperation and resources.

NEW WORK RULE: Collaboration and partnership with your team members is the new normal, and is essential in co-creating transformative ideas and solutions that will lead to more regular and consistent breakthroughs and outcomes.

rule five

CO-DEVELOPMENT

What I learned early on in my career at Merrill was that our fifteen thousand financial advisors could be a real catalyst for change. The power of deep and systemic peer-to-peer coaching can unleash an awesome force of development.

ANDY SIEG, president, Merrill Lynch Wealth Management

I was talking with Jim Collins, author of the business classics *Built to Last* and *Good to Great,* when his study of West Point's culture came up. He recalled how impressed he'd been watching the way cadets helped cheer on, coach, and instruct their fellow cadets working their way through the indoor obstacle course—considered one of the most intense physical challenges at the military academy. Even as the cadets were competing to outdo each other, they also went out of their way to help each other succeed.

Jim learned that this is an important aspect of leadership training at West Point. The cadets supported and encouraged each other because they wanted *everyone* to be better. He also noticed something else about the military academy's cadets: They seemed much happier than students at civilian universities, including Stanford, where he'd taught for seven years. The purpose of West Point is to prepare its cadets to lead, and it's the job of each cadet to help his or her fellow cadets grow and develop their skills. That's the secret to transformational performance for all of us in all organizations. It's the commitment to the shared mission and to each other—to ensure each other's success, to have each other's backs, to coach each other, and to help each other grow and develop. That's the way forward.

During his stay at West Point, Jim noticed that the cadets engaged with him differently than typical college students he'd met. They seemed unusually direct and curious. They asked a lot of questions and let Jim know when they disagreed with him. To me, that seemed like the natural result of West Point's co-elevating environment. Wherever you see people in a high-performance organization engaging honestly and expressing themselves fully, those are surefire signs of a highly supportive coaching culture.

Coaching and mentoring in the workplace are more important today than ever, given how rapidly changing market conditions require individuals and organizations alike to keep reinventing themselves. But tighter budgets, flatter organizations, heavier workloads, and higher numbers of direct reports have left managers stretched too thin. Most are unable to shoulder the important responsibilities of coaching and mentoring the way they themselves were once coached and mentored.

To compound matters, your boss may well be little more than a face you see now and then or only on video, someone who works out of a different building or in another city altogether. (In 2014, FG's research institute surveyed 1,700 knowledge workers and found that 79 percent reported always or frequently working in dispersed teams.) For all these reasons, most workplaces are starved for coaching support.

This rising need, coupled with the coaching vacuum, is why coaching today depends on each of us. Under the new work rules, we have a new contract with our peers, one in which we owe them our candid feedback and solicit their feedback. We each need to take responsibility for coaching and developing the members of our teams, and we need to seek their coaching as well. Peer-to-peer co-development of this kind is at the heart of leading without authority. It's the natural fulfillment of co-elevation. In today's world, if we see one of our teammates falling behind and neglect to give our feedback, that is tantamount to sabotage.

It's easy to use the word "feedback" without recognizing there are three distinct kinds of feedback, and some forms of feedback are easier to give than others. The easiest kind of feedback is idea feedback—helpful co-creational feedback on how to do something better ("Hey, Joe, why not try it this way?"). The feedback that's a little harder to give is performance feedback, because that's about accountability ("Hey, Joe, I think your team can hit higher numbers than last month."). Finally, there's competency feedback, the personalized feedback you give about an individual teammate's abilities. It's not the kind of feedback you can toss around casually with a "Hey, Joe" remark.

All truly impactful coaching happens in this third area of personal competency feedback. Whether we need a specific upgrade in certain hard skills or ongoing coaching in our soft skills, we all need to be told where our competencies need to grow and develop.

DEVELOPMENT IS EVERYONE'S JOB

The original idea for this book was based on a simple premise: Within every relationship, there is an element of mutual coaching, which, if it was purposefully activated, could draw out both parties' highest potential. And yet of all the ideas you see in this book, it is this concept, of peer-to-peer coaching, of *co-development,* that draws the most skepticism and pushback.

The most common objection I hear is, "It's just not my role. It's not my job." That's certainly true under the traditional rules of work, where coaching was something bosses offered to subordinates, and subordinates were expected to comply with it.

The other objection I hear, even from those who like the idea of peer-to-peer co-development, is that the risk of hurt feelings and strained relationships with the people we have to work with every day is too much to bear. Most people can't bring themselves to tell a colleague he has spinach in his teeth, let alone offer personal feedback on how that colleague could improve his skills in listening, communication, prioritizing, or time management. Either we don't feel we have the permission to give such intimate feedback, or, more likely, we'd rather play it safe. We value being liked more than we value helping a colleague, helping the team meet its goals, or helping the company's mission. We want to be *nice.*

In her groundbreaking bestseller *Radical Candor,* my friend Kim Scott gives a pretty brutal name to this brand of nice. She calls it manipulative insincerity—when you don't challenge your colleague, because, ultimately, you don't care about him or the mission. It's the absolute opposite of radical candor, which is all about challenging because you care.[1]

I admit that it's easier to slide into manipulative insincerity and avoid difficult conversations. But then I think back to Jim Collins's West Point experiences. How can you claim to care about the mission and your teammates without offering personal feedback and coaching? Where's the integrity in refusing to get involved when a teammate is struggling with a problem? There is none. The new rules of work mandate that we engage our teammates, that we be of service to them. In Kim Scott's terms, we care about them, we challenge them, we give them the gift of our radical candor. For those leading others without authority, as with any kind of leadership, this is a primary obligation.

If these ideas make you nervous, consider this: You're already in some form of co-developing relationship with the people closest to you. Look at your relationship with your spouse or significant other, or your relationships with your friends, siblings, parents, children. To one degree or another, we routinely try to offer advice to and help those we're closest to in terms of growth and self-development. Why? Because we care about them, and they care about us.

Everyone has experience providing candid feedback in a spirit of generosity and goodwill. You might just not have done it in the workplace. Whatever resistance you may be feeling, be candid with yourself about the source of your fear.

Is your fear of conflict or of hurting someone's feelings nothing more than manipulative insincerity on your part? If you genuinely care about your colleagues, your teams, and the goals and mission of the organization, don't you have an obligation to speak up? Isn't that what real leaders do? Maybe you have a blind spot about how to engage the challenges of the new work world and need to be made aware of it.

If you're reading this book, I doubt you are someone who consciously engages in manipulative insincerity. But perhaps you are doing so unconsciously at times, without being fully aware of it. If so, recognizing when you do that is a valuable breakthrough for you. It's the first area where you need to request some peer-to-peer development.

> When we added "Learn and Be Curious" to Amazon's leadership principles, it was to emphasize the idea that leaders are never done learning and always seek to improve themselves. Leaders can't afford to grow complacent in these fast-changing times, and need to remain focused on improving what works and fixing what doesn't. Building collaborative relationships within our increasingly networked work environment helps tap into our curiosity and encourages us to learn from a diverse group of colleagues.
>
> JEFF WILKE, CEO Worldwide Consumer, Amazon

IT'S ALL IN HOW YOU SAY IT

Years ago, I coached the leadership team at the struggling subsidiary of a large and respected tech and media conglomerate. While I was there, Daphne, the COO, helped lead a turnaround of the division, thanks to the close co-developing relationship she developed with Carter, the CFO.

Together, Carter and Daphne had each other's backs. She coached him regularly on his choice of words and even his body language in meetings with the extended team. They discussed his tendency to be abrupt or project an air of indifference. And Carter appreciated Daphne's feedback. He, in turn, coached Daphne about her leadership communications style and her presence in staff meetings. He gave her tips on how to be clearer and more deliberate in expressing her opinions, and how to keep to the agenda and hold everyone responsible for next steps.

Over the course of one particularly challenging year, the two of them moved forward as a united front, and as a result succeeded in getting the organization's sales and marketing efforts turned around. The company reversed what had been a years-long decline, and at last found a path to profitability.

What's striking about their story is how Daphne and Carter got to this point. Their relationship had not started out this way. At best, they had had a coexisting relationship, one where they tolerated each other but were hardly supportive. Daphne had been hired by the CEO to bring management discipline to a subsidiary that was the worst performer in the parent company's portfolio—it was missing its numbers by as much as 30 percent per year.

When Daphne met Carter, he struck her as a difficult senior executive who seemed more eager to toe the parent-company line than to genuinely improve the business. As she saw it, his frequent recommendations for across-the-board budget cuts lacked the detailed insights and passionate curiosity required to manage a real operational turnaround.

Although Carter seemed like an unlikely candidate for co-elevation, Daphne realized that she could not succeed in her job without him. Like it or not, Carter was on her team. Despite all the visible signs that Carter wouldn't be interested in a co-elevating relationship, she made an effort to get to know him better, personally and professionally, and build a partnership with him. In doing so, she developed more empathy and understanding for the difficulties of his position as a divisional CFO. Gradually, they began to work together more closely on the turnaround, and over time developed a respectful mutually supportive co-elevating relationship.

But there was one big roadblock: No one else on the executive team liked or trusted Carter. Too often, when he met with his colleagues, he behaved like an outside consultant sent to guard the parent company's money. He was dismissive of certain market realities in their industry, such as the competitive pricing pressures the team faced every day. He liked to give moralizing mini lectures to other senior managers about fiduciary responsibility when discussing missed revenue targets and budget overruns. He was sometimes downright dismissive of proposals for spending money on certain strategic investments that could speed the turnaround. Even his body language seemed to communicate that he wasn't interested in what anyone else had to say.

It was clear to Daphne that Carter's dismal relationships with the other executives were undermining the team's mission. Some team members confided to Daphne that they avoided candid conversations with Carter and even withheld sharing sensitive materials with him. At first, Daphne tried coaching them on how to interact with Carter, but she saw that there was not enough transparency and candor—enough porosity—between Carter and the others for them to have constructive conversations.

By nature, Daphne disliked dealing with conflict, but in this case, she had to take charge of the situation. She realized that if she was going to help save the company, she had to mend the relationship between Carter and key members of the leadership team. Co-development is a two-sided endeavor, but she knew it was up to her to take the initiative. Carter needed to change his behavior, and Daphne would have to let him know that in a way that would preserve their relationship—and ideally improve it.

I coached Daphne on how to approach Carter, and I guided her through the seven stages of beginning a co-developing relationship.

1. Ask for Permission and Set a Time and Place

Before we offer feedback, even if we have opened porosity and the existing relationship is strong, we should always request our team-mate's permission and wait for their verbal assent. It's a request for recontracting in your relationship. If they decline our request, okay, well, you've given them that choice. Try again another time.

That's what Daphne did with Carter. She sent him a carefully worded email in which she told him she wanted to give him some feedback and offered him the option to say no. She didn't get into specifics. She just asked his permission to give feedback on how they were playing out their respective roles in the turnaround. She suggested a time—their next weekly meeting.

She wrote:

Carter, before we wrap up our next meeting, I have some thoughts I would like to pass on that I hope you find beneficial.

Over the years, I've benefited from some incredible insights and advice, not just from managers but from my peers, colleagues who I knew cared about me becoming the kind of leader they knew I aspired to be. Your feedback has been particularly valuable, and I thank you. This feedback gave me more confidence and helped me to adopt a greater degree of assertiveness. Sometimes, I thought their feedback was off the mark, and I discounted that particular advice. But I always knew that what they were telling me took courage, and was done with my best interests at heart, and I appreciated it.

If you're open to it, I'd like to offer the same kind of support. If not, that's OK, I completely understand. Let me know.

This is the language to use. The approach is careful, but it's not overly diplomatic BS. It's purposeful without being accusatory. The opening is an expression of caring: "I have thoughts that you might find beneficial." The middle section expresses Daphne's own vulnerability, and how she has benefited from this kind of feedback in the past. And in closing, she makes it clear the decision is up to Carter, giving him complete control over the outcome of the conversation—or whether the conversation will even happen. She explicitly requests his permission, which he is free to decline.

Whether or not you have a formal management title, my advice is to never assume you have permission to coach just because of your position or rank. Even if you're the boss and you have a title that on paper grants you the authority to deliver candid feedback however you like, you still need to first ask permission to offer it. And you need to explain why you're offering it, or it won't land the way you want it to. And it won't accomplish your goals in the long run. No one will listen to your advice unless they trust you, and to gain that trust, you need to request permission to offer feedback, while expressing your commitment to the other person's growth and success.

As it happened, Carter responded just as Daphne had hoped. He wrote back, "Sure. Bring it on. Sounds auspicious." The two had worked collaboratively for so long that it would have been easy for Daphne to assume she'd already earned this permission. But it was still important for her to start by asking. Without our teammates' explicit consent, we have no idea if they're truly open to our feedback.

2. Focus on the Future and Give Them Power

Critiquing past performance often results in the other person feeling the need to defend their actions and choices. When coaching a peer who does not have to take your advice, I find the most productive approach is to keep coaching feedback focused on the future, and on what someone can do going forward to be more successful. If you find you must look in the rearview mirror to identify counterproductive past behaviors, then also be sure to praise and celebrate positive past behaviors that you'll want to encourage in the future.

Avoid saying what they should or must do. The phrase "You might" is much better. It's a generous suggestion, indicating that they're free to do with your feedback what they wish. Use conciliatory language like, "What I really appreciated about our partnership last quarter was XYZ, and for next quarter, I might suggest we try ABC."

Avoid the pitfall of sounding as though you are trying to exercise control over them or their actions, especially if you have no formal authority over them at all. One of the reasons most of us are so resistant to feedback is that years of instruction from parents and bosses have conditioned us to believe we must take it, that feedback must come with corrective action. Instead, you are merely trying to serve the mission and your teammate by offering feedback that will help both of you go higher together. It's one of the biggest differences between co-development and traditional managerial feedback.

At their next one-on-one, Daphne waited until they had wrapped up their work to broach the feedback she wanted to offer. "Carter . . ." she began. Carter abruptly interrupted her. "I know," he said. "I'm coming off as a jerk to the executive team."

"Well, I wouldn't have put it so bluntly," she said. "But . . . sometimes, yeah."

Daphne was both surprised and relieved. The open-ended language in her note had given Carter some time to think about and prepare for what Daphne had to say. Resisting anything that might be construed as piling on, she switched the subject to the future as quickly as she could.

"I've deeply appreciated our newfound partnership," she said. "We're laying the groundwork for what seems to be becoming a powerful transformation of the executive team and the company." To get there, she told him, the team dynamics needed to change as well. "I believe you have an opportunity to model that change for them," she said.

Then she drew on what she'd learned about preparing the other person to hear candid feedback. "Okay, so we're clear, these are just my opinions," she began. "You're free to do with them as you will. Accept, modify, or ignore them. The advice is yours to evaluate. The way I see it, we have an opportunity to develop greater trust between you and the other executives on the team. If we don't, I fear it's going to limit your ability to break through with them and work collaboratively to turn things around. What do you think?"

Daphne paused. Her open-ended question allowed Carter to weigh in with his take before she went too far down the road of how to increase trust on the team.

Carter's brow was furrowed. He looked down and rubbed his temples. " 'Trust' is a powerful word. Are you saying the team doesn't trust me?" he asked, sounding a bit defensive.

Without mentioning names, Daphne told him that some team members were avoiding speaking with him and had been withholding information from him. "I don't believe for a moment that your intention is to alienate any of the others on the team," she said. "Actions don't always convey intentions," she acknowledged, "and misunderstandings in changing the direction of a company of our size happen all the time." She used her own experience as an example. In her efforts to please Gavin, the CEO, she said, "I've been perceived by some as just an administrator, rather than a strategic leader. Trust me, that wasn't easy to hear when someone on the team brought it to my attention."

Carter listened intently, but still looked wounded. "Trust and integrity are important, core values of mine, particularly in finance," he said. "I'm hurt that I'm not seen as trustworthy. And if the team really doesn't trust me, I'm not sure that's an easy thing to overcome."

Daphne shook her head. "I believe there are a few simple actions you can take that would begin to address the trust issue. I'm happy to talk through those with you, if you are open to hearing them. And again, these are just my observations."

Carter thanked her. "Honestly, what you're saying comes as a surprise," he said. "I'm going to have to sit and digest it. If I want or need your input or help, I'll let you know."

3. Welcome Their Feedback

To keep the thread of the conversation going, Daphne said, "On a selfish note, at our next meeting, will you share any reflections you have for me that can help the turnaround? I value your insights and opinions."

I urge you never to deliver personal feedback without requesting it in return. The term is *co*-development. It's a two-way street. Daphne wanted Carter to see that she too had blind spots, that she too could benefit from *his* coaching—and that she was open to it. She also wanted to show Carter that she viewed his insights about her performance as valuable, and welcome.

Remember, even if we are leading the team, we are never above anyone on the team. We're right there on the ground beside our teammates, continuing to grow and develop with them. We set the standards in our engagement with them. Moreover, we really do want their candid feedback, differing perspectives, and coaching.

Offering caring candor becomes easier with time as we build psychological safety and open porosity among our teammates. Notice that I said "easier," not easy. No matter how strong the bond among team members, these conversations can be tough. They are intensely personal. But if we stick to these rules, then we'll be paving the way for successful co-development.

4. Let It Go: Feedback Is a Gift. Once Given, It's Theirs.

When Daphne delivered her feedback to Carter, she assured him that what he did with the information was up to him. In that sense, coaching feedback is truly a gift. Once you've given the gift of feedback, it becomes the other person's property. It's for them to consume, consider, analyze—or discard.

As Daphne explicitly told Carter, "I'm offering these thoughts because I care about you and our team. But I don't have any expectations or preconceptions as to what you should do with them, or what happens next." She didn't want Carter to feel defensive or compelled to act on her feedback. She wanted him to understand that he was in full control.

In the following weeks, Daphne was careful not to make references to their conversation about team trust when they met. Daphne didn't know when or even if Carter would ever bring it up again.

Three weeks after their initial talk, Carter asked if they could follow up on what she'd told him, before their regular weekly meeting began. He explained to her why her comments had come as a shock to him. The other executives, he said, didn't understand how hard he worked to sell the corporate CFO on the turnaround plan. "I put my reputation on the line," he said. "Sometimes it feels like the only way I can get the executive team's and the employees' attention is to have corporate light a fire under them."

Listening to him, Daphne realized for the first time that Carter was genuinely unaware of the impact his behavior was having on the company's turnaround plan. Departments suffering in the volatile marketplace needed to work closely with the CFO to identify efficiencies, not struggle with the added burden of clumsy across-the-board budget cuts. Perhaps due in part to the increased candor of their conversations, Daphne was surprised to feel even more empathy for Carter than before.

Again, since our feedback is a gift, we must be prepared for the possibility that our teammate may not accept it. As with an ugly tie from Aunt Ginny at Christmas, they have the right to thank us and put it in a drawer without ever trying it on. Your job is to humbly offer to help someone with the issues and concerns they are facing, not force them into a response. If they don't want or accept your gift, then you have to let go. Accept them for who they are and where they are on their personal and career development journey. Work with them up to the limits of their ability, and keep trying to reach out to them at the level of permission you have earned.

If you don't let go, if you attempt to control or manipulate their behavior, you'll find yourself constantly battling them. As a result, you might push them away and make them resistant to co-development. You may find they won't want to be part of your team at all. Instead, give your teammates the space they need to choose their own path, with your support.

5. Lead Them to Discovery

Candid feedback doesn't always have to be so direct. Follow-up can be more subtle and nuanced, especially when you have been engaged in the coaching conversation for a while. Ask questions that help your teammate reflect on their performance and behavior. Help them find the answers by being authentically curious and interested in exploring questions and answers together.

Daphne noted Carter's initial defensiveness and how he didn't believe he was at fault. But she also heard him acknowledge that there was a problem to be addressed. She felt that acknowledgment of responsibility might have created a window she could use to be more direct in her feedback.

"I wonder if we can come up with a few simple suggestions to try going forward," she told Carter. "Perhaps you and I could use more language like 'we' and 'us' with the team so they know that we think everyone belongs to the same team. We might ask, 'What can we do to better support your sales efforts?' instead of just quizzing them about poor outcomes.

"They may decline the offer," she told him, "but we'll get points for offering."

Daphne also had some practical suggestions for making Carter come across as more of a team player. "Let's ask to be involved in solutions," she told him. "When you're running financial projections or you've discovered that our numbers are off, consider bringing that information to me and Gavin first before sharing it with corporate. That will give our team time to gather their thoughts before being asked to explain—without violating company procedures."

And then Daphne attempted to set their joint vision on the future. "It may not seem like much, but making these kinds of small changes in how you show up will go a long way to making you a part of 'us' and not 'them.'"

To me, Daphne was making an important point. Even when we feel we haven't earned permission to give direct, candid feedback, we can always use language that helps our teammates discover their own truths. Here's where asking questions and inviting them to reflect on past failures and successes can help them see their behavior and come to their own insights.

Try asking "what" and "how" questions. For example, let's say you were part of a negotiation that you think was badly botched. Peter led the negotiation and was so eager to close the deal that he made a lot of concessions the customer didn't even ask for. In other words, Peter just gave away a lot of the company's money. But you may not have permission to offer that kind of critical feedback. Instead, try asking "what" and "how" questions that steer the conversation in that direction: "What do you think about that negotiation?

How could we have done better? How did you perform in previous negotiations? What was it that made that last negotiation successful? Do you feel this one was different?"

These kinds of questions lead our teammates to draw their own conclusions. And as a result, they are much more likely to generate their own aha moments. When we ask questions that lead our teammates to work out these issues for themselves, we're giving them a gift that leads to the most powerful and lasting form of personal growth and development.

Meanwhile, avoid questions that ask "why." They can come off as judgmental, and rarely lead to constructive conversation. I know, because I used to ask "why" questions all the time. I thought I was being candid. I really did want to get to the bottom of why something had gone wrong—a missed date, a project that fell behind budget or schedule, a decision that turned out badly. But in doing so, I came off sounding accusatory. I wasn't demonstrating my understanding or support of the other person, or the team, and the question didn't get me the answers I was looking for.

A question that is essentially framed as, "Why did you send Peter in to lead that negotiation when he has so little experience?" will make the entire team feel interrogated. A much better approach is to ask, "What are your thoughts about how Peter led that negotiation?" Now you're asking for their feedback and advice, which makes them less defensive. They no longer feel obliged to explain and justify their decisions.

6. Care, Care, Then Care Some More

So much in the opening stages of a co-developing relationship depends upon tone, approach, language, and, above all, genuine caring. You really have to care about the other person to create a co-elevating relationship. Daphne didn't want Carter to change just to suit her needs. She knew that her team's complaints about Carter reflected poorly on him as an executive. For his own sake, he needed to know why he was failing with them.

Daphne frequently began her feedback with praise, and then followed up with candid feedback. This contradicts everything my former coach, Morrice, taught me (sorry, Morrice!). She would call this a "shit sandwich," and say that putting two slices of bread around a slice of criticism doesn't make it easier to swallow.

Now, if you don't really care about the other person's development, then Morrice was right. But there is one big difference between a "shit sandwich" and a sincere co-elevating conversation: authentic concern. If you have criticism to give, always make sure your authentic concern shines through in the course of the conversation. Again, no one cares how much you know until they know how much you care.

7. Set the Expectation of Accountability

Daphne and Carter's weekly meeting was a reliable structure to ensure their accountability to each other in their co-development. While Carter didn't circle back for more advice on this particular matter, Daphne saw that her feedback had gotten through to him. And he did reach out to her when he came across an unexpected hiccup in their financials, instead of going to corporate immediately. She also witnessed him mirroring with the team the language she used with him. Before they gave joint updates during team meetings, she'd intentionally pepper her speech with words like "we" and "us" to stress the point that they were all on the same team. And Carter, perhaps in response, always followed suit.

Look, you may need to move forward more deliberately. When your teammate gives you their feedback, ask them to hold *you* accountable in real time, and/or request a monthly or biweekly check-in.

Here's how to ask for *real-time accountability* when someone has given you feedback:

Thanks, Joe, I would love to jump on that and make some changes in how I listen to others, as you suggested. Do me a favor. If you see me talking over people or interrupting, you have total permission to call me on it on the spot.

If you realize you might be defensive if someone does that to you in front of others, then give the other person a slightly amended version of that guidance.

> Hey, Joe, I would love to jump on that and make some changes in how I listen to others, as you suggested. Do me a favor. If you see me talking over people or interrupting, could you pull me aside right after and point it out?

If you sense you are going to be defensive but realize the real-time feedback will help you change your behavior, then try suggesting a safe word or phrase that the other person can use as a kind of code. Make it light and fun.

> So, here's the thing, Joe. I would love to jump on that and make some changes in how I listen to others, as you suggested. But gosh, when I get rolling, it's tough to stop, particularly if I'm heated up or excited about something. Pull me aside after the meeting, by all means, but even in the moment, try to get my attention by saying something like, "I wonder what the team is thinking." When I hear that, I totally promise to slow down. I realize I'm a work in progress, and I really appreciate your willingness to help me be at the top of my game. And of course, I'm happy to return the favor if I can help you at some point.

Setting a regular biweekly or monthly check-in can be invaluable. Ask your teammate if they'd give you a progress update on whatever behavior you're seeking to change. At each check-in, offer to give them feedback in return. The longer it takes for someone to ask for feedback, the better prepared you need to be with specific, easy-to-execute examples. And the more empathic you need to be when delivering it. In the case of someone who is tentative about receiving feedback, you might attempt a trial balloon, something easy, to help them get over their fear of hearing feedback, and as a result start to ask for it more regularly. Typically, by the second check-in, most people are likely to accept your offer. And now you're really co-developing.

I can't imagine a meaningful and productive relationship where candid feedback wasn't at the core and the foundation to building trust. Leaders should make it known that candid feedback is expected regularly as part of your operating norms. Visibly demonstrating openness to alternate viewpoints will foster a culture that makes it safe to constructively disagree and seek new approaches to innovation.

JEFF MIRVISS, president,
Peripheral Interventions, Boston Scientific

CO-DEVELOPMENT: THE ULTIMATE FORM OF SERVICE

Daphne's approach was one of *caring candor*. She wasn't trying to be mean by pointing out to Carter that the team didn't trust him. Nor was she indulging her emotions by hurling feedback at him defensively or aggressively to demean, belittle, or offend him. She shared what she had experienced directly, without emotion or embellishment, because she genuinely believed Carter's success was critical to the success of the team and their mission.

Drawing on caring candor will help you to help your teammates grow, learn, and develop. I've found it is the most effective way to invite someone to be receptive to feedback. We tend to tune out criticism when it is dished out by someone who only seems to want to point out what we did wrong. But when we give feedback out of a spirit of truly wanting to help the other person become the best they can possibly be, it is the ultimate form of generosity. You are genuinely serving them.

Co-development is the sort of gift that can last a lifetime, forever changing the trajectory of someone's personal and professional life. This single conversation changed the course of Daphne's and Carter's lives. And it can do the same for you and those you care about. Here are a few tips on expressing caring candor.

Be Present

To cultivate the level of trust required to be a great coach, it's crucial to listen with complete focus and care. "There is always an energetic connection when people come together," writes Marcia Reynolds in her book *The Discomfort Zone*. "Something happens in the space 'between brains' when people interact. Your intention for the conversation, your emotions, and your regard for the person will impact their willingness, desire, and courage to change. You have to stay present and aware to sustain trust throughout the conversation."[2]

As I write this, my phone lies next to me. Every thirty minutes, I check my texts. I should turn off the phone; better still, I should put it in the other room. I don't. When you're offering face-to-face development, however, you *must* give your teammate your full, undivided attention. In 2012, *Time* magazine asked, "Is Your Cell Phone Making You a Jerk?" The article cited studies showing the intimate connection between trust and being fully present, and how even a short period of cell phone use can break that connection, making people less empathetic to and conscious of others.[3]

If you make the effort to bring a colleague to the table to develop trust and build a better rapport together, don't blow it by being distracted.

Make Sure Your Feedback Is for Them *and Not You*

Coaching often fails when it's more about the person giving it than the person receiving it. Make sure the feedback you provide is for your *teammate* and not for you. Check yourself before you say something that might be taken as criticism. Ask yourself, "How will what I'm about to say serve them?" And if you're still not sure, ask someone else.

There was a sales associate at our technology company who was excellent in many ways, but I strongly believed she needed to polish her personal presentation. The way she dressed, her etiquette, her grammar, and even her speaking tone needed to improve if she wanted to advance and play a more significant role in selling our products and services to the top HR executives in the world.

In the back of my mind, though, I wondered, "Maybe I'm just being overly sensitive." I felt concerned that I might be projecting some of my own issues onto her. Growing up on the other side of the tracks and attending private schools on scholarship, I was teased mercilessly by the other kids at school for the way I spoke, for not knowing which fork to use, and for the hand-me-down clothes I wore. The last thing I wanted to do was start a conversation that would leave hurt feelings and make this young woman feel the way I used to feel when I was teased.

So before I said anything that might embarrass her, I got some of my HR friends' candid assessment of the feedback I planned to offer. And to my relief, they assured me that I was right, that her current attire and demeanor were bound to limit her career mobility. Armed with the confidence that my feedback was indeed for her advancement (and not because of my own insecurities), I was able to broach the delicate subject with her, after asking her permission to do so, and she took my feedback in the spirit it was given.

I learned to be mindful of this issue at an unlikely place: Al-Anon. Although Al-Anon was created as a support group for people whose lives have been affected by a loved one's drinking, many people attend Al-Anon meetings to deal with any number of situations that are beyond their control. When I first went to Al-Anon, I was dealing with a dysfunctional relationship, and needed to recognize that I could not control the other person's behavior, despite how much I tried. I immediately saw parallels in the relationships I had with some of my employees, as well. In retrospect, my disapproval of any given behavior was prompted by how that behavior made me feel personally disrespected. My ego was invested in the other person's change. I wanted them to change *for me* instead of for themselves.

So when we deliver candid feedback, we have to be sure that our ego is not involved, and that the concern is positioned around what we know people want for themselves. I can hear myself telling my son when he was younger, "Stop chewing your food with your mouth open." Upon my reprimand, I usually saw a slight modification of his behavior, but one that was never sustained. On another occasion, I delivered the same feedback in a different way: "Remember that girl at school you talk about? Do you eat like this around her?"

This time he stopped, leaned in, and asked, "What do you mean?" I explained that girls tend to care a little more about hygiene and good manners than most boys at his age. By positioning the advice as being of service to him and his desire to be liked by girls, he became more interested in it.

Try Asking for Coaching Before Offering to Coach Others

Ideally, co-development is like a tennis match. Sometimes we serve and sometimes we receive service. We offer candid feedback to our teammates when needed, they offer feedback to us, and back and forth we go. But when we're just starting out, sharing our candid feedback about a teammate's performance is often too daunting. If you sense that you haven't earned enough permission to do so, then don't. Try *first* asking your teammate to help *you* develop. Then later, if the exchange has gone well, weave in an offer to do so in return.

You may not even need to do that very often. In general, when we make a habit of asking for other people's opinions, they're much more likely to solicit our opinions. Feedback works the same way. If you are known to ask for feedback frequently from everyone on the team, it's very likely that many of them will invite you to give feedback in return.

And if you suspect you're past the point of needing development— think again. Everyone at every level benefits from it. "Never stop learning," Indra Nooyi, former chairman and CEO of PepsiCo, once told *Fortune* magazine. "Whether you're an entry level employee fresh out of college or a CEO, you don't know it all. Admitting this is not a sign of weakness. The strongest leaders are those who are life-long students."[4]

Own How Your Candor Lands

Just because you've earned the permission to offer candid feedback doesn't mean you can assume it's always welcome. Even when we have established a solid foundation of trust, and candor rules the day in our relationships, it's still easy to overstep.

I was working with a new team recently, and one of the members of the team stated up front, almost as a warning, that they were very candid by nature; that's just how they were made.

They were using that claim as a badge of pride, but I soon found it was just a pretext for disruptive behavior. Several times during the meeting, this person made it clear he didn't agree with the solution we were discussing and didn't think it was worth further consideration. He showed an utter lack of curiosity in what others were saying, and at one point, his comments grew so hostile that they shut down the conversation entirely.

Later I learned a little about this disruptive team member's background. He'd had a pretty tough upbringing, in a home where his opinions were always dismissed, so he developed a habit of rushing to get in his two cents whenever he could. As an adult, he rebranded his "insecure little boy" behaviors as "candid guy who just says it like it is." But this kind of scorched-earth-style candor never works, because everyone on the receiving end knows what's really going on: This person is not putting the shared mission first.

As givers of feedback, we must own how our candor lands. We must offer our candor and feedback in ways that are meant to foster dialogue—not to win arguments. It's just lazy and self-indulgent to care so little about the viewpoints of others that you assume they will accept your point of view on your terms. And that hurts your efforts to advance the team's mission and goals.

Meanwhile, it's worth noting that we all have behaviors held over from our earlier lives that no longer serve us very well. This is why we need our teammates to be courageous and caring co-developers who will help us align our behaviors with all the things we really want in life.

Avoid Defensiveness

When I was a CMO, I used to pay a lot of money for research reports on what others thought about our services. I would have been an idiot to get those reports and put them in a drawer without reading them. In the same way, we'd be fools if we chose not to hear what others think about us and kept doing what we do with no concern for other perspectives.

Hearing our weaknesses articulated or our poor performance called out tends to trigger defensiveness in most of us. To help combat this very common challenge, here are some of the best practices I've found to help better hear and embrace feedback.

Stay calm. Try to remember that feedback is nothing more than data in service of everyone going higher. Remind yourself that you control what you do with that data. Consider it a gift, even if it hurts, and do your best to receive with humility and grace whatever feedback your teammate offers you.

We always have a choice when it comes to indulging negative emotions and letting them get the best of us. Yes, controlling emotions is easier for some people than others, but it's essential to recognize that shutting down others' feedback through your defensiveness and other emotional responses will limit your potential growth.

Some people struggle with feedback because they think it's actually a directive they have to follow. That's a holdover from the days when managers ruled by fiat. But it is not true. You have the right to assess whether the feedback will help you become a more effective team member. That said, it's essential for your professional growth and success that you don't miss out on the powerful potential insights and course correction that can come from caring feedback.

And if you just can't control your emotions and are having a hard time receiving criticism and feedback, then air out the issue with your co-elevating partners—and work on it together. *Remember, you are in control.* You can change your response. You can remain open to criticism, if you choose to.

Ask questions. With defensiveness taken off the table, curiosity can emerge front and center. Be excited to explore what you are told. If you don't understand the feedback or it's unclear, ask for clarification. Be careful not to sound defensive. If your teammate's feedback is too general, dive deeper—but do it with excitement. For instance, if the other person says, "You would benefit from dialing up your communication skills," ask for more detailed feedback: "Do I speak too much during meetings? Is my tone off? Do I sound disrespectful? If I had to focus on just one thing, what would that be?" Responses like, "I'd love to understand that better," or "Oh, thanks, can you give me an example of a time you felt that?" invite candor and signal your maturity and openness to grow and develop.

Say "thank you." Whether or not you agree with the feedback, always thank your teammate as you would thank anyone for a gift. Be clear that you will put the gift of their feedback in the mix as you collect additional feedback. Acknowledge their generosity. This helps build even greater trust and psychological safety between the two of you and keeps the porosity between you open. Invite them to keep sharing their perspective or insights. Even on occasions when we feel like someone is deliberately using feedback to make a personal dig at us, we can't take the bait. We need to take the high road instead by just saying "thank you."

It's always better to know what your teammates think. Then you are in control of what to do with the information. The alternative is to be isolated, guessing what others are thinking and feeling mystified or even victimized by some of their actions.

Don't pump the well dry. The stronger the relationship, the more fluid and frequent the feedback can, and should, be. So, after advocating for more feedback, be mindful how often *you* ask for it in return. Gauge the level of the other person's investment in you. You be the judge, based on how much porosity you have developed, to what degree you and your co-elevating partner are committed to each other and to going higher together, and how much your team's project or goals or mission demands it.

Seek Feedback on Your Feedback

Once the back and forth of feedback is a habit and a natural way of working, it's a good idea to refine your exchanges by seeking feedback on how you give feedback. This is the time to inquire how the feedback you are sharing with the other person is landing. You or your teammates may wish to dial up or down aspects of your feedback based on their perception of its impact on people. This kind of open dialogue is healthy and can deepen your partnership as you go higher together.

What doesn't work is expecting the other person to be a mind reader, or to know intuitively how you prefer to collaborate, receive feedback, or communicate. One of my personal challenges is that I often push for action quickly and definitively. If I've got a half hour, I want to get to the point and know we have used our time productively. Our head of marketing at FG, on the other hand, really appreciates the intimacy of having longer conversations. She takes enormous pride in our work and wants to discuss the steps that went into how we arrived at a decision or point of view. The result is that sometimes, during a conversation, I'll interrupt her to tell her to get to the point, and she'll shut down, hurt by my impatience.

For our co-elevation relationship to work, I needed to avoid feeling frustrated and she needed to avoid feeling underappreciated or disrespected. We needed to understand each other's thinking and fine-tune our approach. I worked on achieving more empathy for how she prefers to communicate, tried to express that to her, and guarded against expressing impatience when she was speaking. Our mutual candidness and intention to work as a team has helped us both to recognize the merits of our different styles. Ultimately, it has helped make our work with others more fun, fluid, and effective.

Our teammates aren't Vulcan mind readers. We need to help

them understand us, and request that we coach each other in working together.

> Team leaders often think they are being "kind" by not sharing feedback that will hurt someone's feelings, but kindness requires the courage to be candid. It's easy to confuse kindness with weakness, but true kindness requires strength. High-performance environments rely on candor and transparency, because that's what it takes to create rich, collaborative partnerships that produce extraordinary results.
>
> DANIEL LUBETZKY, CEO, KIND Snacks

Co-Develop with Your Boss

I'm often asked whether we should try to offer candid personal feedback to our bosses, and my answer is always "Absolutely!" The higher people move up the corporate ladder, the more they need feedback from those under them—and the less likely they are to get it.

In the military, people are trained to give open feedback to those who rank above them by first saying, "Permission to speak freely, sir?" At one of my companies, an executive who was a former Army Ranger actually carried over that practice to his corporate career. Whenever he approached me with those magic words, I knew I was in for a double helping of sincere, caring criticism.

The natural concern, though, is that your actual feedback won't be well received. What if your boss gets upset? If that happens, apologize, and suggest that you were offering your humble thoughts because you care enough to do so.

It's also possible that you haven't earned permission to offer feedback. Your boss may not be open or ready to hear what you have to say, until you get him or her ready. Opening up porosity is on you. Work on building that permission, returning to the practices of serve, share, and, most important, care.

To be sure, there are managers who are domineering and controlling, with zero self-awareness. In the end, it's also on you to be careful when reading the room. Don't step over the line and unnecessarily provoke your boss. Keep your job. Or then again, start looking for a new one. You most likely will be better off.

Start a Peer-to-Peer Coaching Movement

In 2017, when Merrill Lynch CEO Andy Sieg announced a renewed focus on revenue growth, a veteran advisor named Richard Pluta reached out to his friend Steve Samuels at Merrill's headquarters to see how he could help.

Together Rich and Steve brought a plan to Andy that, at its core, entailed inviting consistently top-growing Merrill Lynch's advisors to start up the Advisor Growth Network (AGN), a community for all advisors to coach each other and share the high-growth techniques that had put them at the very top.

"It was time we stepped up and took responsibility for ourselves and each other," Rich said. "Who better to jumpstart a program like this than the team members themselves? Today we have initiated a movement and together we are motivating and inspiring each other as we develop our ability to serve our clients and grow our business."

Soon, the AGN had more than six hundred members from among the company's fifteen thousand advisors. Today, there are coaching groups in local Merrill Lynch offices, supporting the growth of their peers by coaching each other while also getting coaching from those with proven track records.

When the firm's regional market executives saw the early results of the AGN efforts, they decided to create co-elevating development teams to share their managerial best practices, and leverage the same FG co-elevation approach. The results since then have been amazing. In just the first two years, Merrill Lynch reported a six-fold increase in the rate of household acquisitions, with revenues, net flows, and net income hitting all-time records.

With the AGN as the foundation, followed by the manager level and then regional office peer-to-peer coaching, Sieg's growth plan is working. Rich, Steve, the AGN members, and soon thousands of local-office members of the growth movement will be helping themselves and helping the company by throwing their shoulders behind the common mission of accelerated growth and increased client care.

A CO-DEVELOPING PARTNERSHIP

Over time, Carter's requests for Daphne's feedback grew more frequent. During their meeting prep, he'd ask, "Is it okay to say this?" She'd candidly explain, "This is what I hear you saying . . . ," or "You might want to consider saying . . ."

Coaching Carter proved to be a growth opportunity for Daphne as well. She grew as a leader and learned how sometimes, it's best to let small things pass. Daphne disliked how Carter felt compelled to script every line of his presentations. He came off as so dry and robotic. She suggested instead that in his next presentation, he simply refer casually to written bullet points. But when Carter tried it, he was so noticeably uncomfortable that the presentation went over poorly. On reflection, Daphne realized that Carter's presentation style didn't really matter. She adjusted her feedback to Carter's needs and abilities and became a better coach as a result.

Daphne was always generous with praise of Carter in front of the team, to remind them all how far he'd come and how much progress they were making together. She was mindful to follow up each meeting with a text to Carter to let him know how much she appreciated his hard work, or to say how grateful she was to have his financial acumen and scenario analysis. Before each meeting, she took a moment to reflect on Carter's contribution to her, the team, and the company. And she freely told him ways she saw him changing and building a better rapport with the team.

With their division in trouble, Daphne and Carter wasted no time putting their trusting co-developing relationship to work. They began inviting other key members from their executive team to their lunches in the cafeteria. Discussions and co-creations and many CPS questions with sales leaders generated new ideas that resulted in more focused and reasonable near-term sales targets. In one luncheon, Daphne and Carter were surprised to learn how a fundamentally different mix of products could generate cost savings for the company, which Carter could never have imagined from his financial perspective alone.

Daphne and Carter worked with the sales leaders to establish a set of iterative thirty-day "winning sprints," each designed to show measurable achievements while also giving the team time to adapt and change course when needed. When some critical targets were missed at the end of the first sprint, the heads of HR and sales requested more funding for sales training. Carter resisted at first, then relented after sitting in on a training session, where he could see for himself the value of training.

These informal little cafeteria meetings convened by Daphne and Carter soon moved to Gavin's conference room, and the group size expanded to six or eight in each session. Daphne and Carter each built relationship action plans so they could expand their team more formally. What began as casual, informal data-gathering conversations between them and the other members of the team evolved into collaborative problem-solving sessions.

In this way, Daphne and Carter's co-development inevitably opened the door to transformative co-creation throughout the executive team. In one of their CPS sessions, the legal counsel's casual observation about contract terms led to an amazing breakthrough. Two simple changes in the sales contract language boosted renewal rates by 30 percent in a single forty-five-day stretch. Sales made its quarterly targets for the first time in five years.

Wins like these provided energy to the team's efforts, and over a series of months, a new strategic plan emerged based on improved credit management, new acquisitions, and a new go-to-market model. Not everyone could keep up with the pace, so Gavin made some long overdue leadership changes at the top in IT and marketing—moves he made with the help of Daphne's coaching. By the time my coaching with the executive team was complete, the company had achieved profitability for the first time in more than five years.

All these amazing organizational wins were rooted in Daphne's recognition that Carter was her team member and needed her coaching. She accepted that it was all on her to co-elevate with Carter and create an intimate, trusting co-developing relationship with him. And then, because the two of them had each other's backs, they were able to overcome setback after setback as they collaborated with their colleagues and fulfilled their goals.

OLD WORK RULE: When it came to growing professionally and developing both hard and soft skills, you looked to your manager, and to performance reviews and training programs. As a manager yourself, you generally only offered developmental feedback to someone who was formally assigned to you as a direct report.

NEW WORK RULE: We seek out our team for development and growth. We offer teammates the candid feedback they need to develop and improve their skills, performance, and behavior because we are committed to their success and to the success of the greater mission.

WHAT IS TRUST?

Carter was shocked to hear that the other members of the executive team didn't trust him. In his mind, he was extremely trustworthy and of high integrity. Trust was essential to his job. What he came to recognize is that there are different kinds and levels of trust, and trustworthy behavior of one kind doesn't necessarily lead to trust in another area.

Over the years, our research at FG has focused on interventions that actively build trust in service of team performance during periods of transformation, when teams really get stressed. The model of trust we use distinguishes three kinds of trust, the three areas where each type of trust is likely to break down, and how to build it up.

Professional trust is built when work expectations are met. But they can get strained when different points of view arise from different professional experiences. For example, trust faltered when Carter, as the head of finance, didn't recognize the value of various operating investments that others on the team felt were necessary to grow sales. Carter was perceived as being shortsighted and incurious about the company's need to grow the business.

Structural trust is where trust most often splinters in an organization. Hierarchies often allow managers to exercise power over their subordinates and their latitude, especially when they give performance reviews and control career paths to promotion. Many checks and balances in a company exist across functions—from finance to HR to IT—giving one function authority over what another may want to accomplish, just as Carter's finance department oversaw budgets and spending. These structural realities can create trust breakdowns and challenge transparency, undermine psychological safety, and impede the fluid risk-taking required for co-elevation and transformation.

Personal trust is the final type of trust. Developing personal trust is the critical lever for navigating the understandable breakdowns of professional and structural trust. It is the trump card for repairing and restoring breakdowns in professional trust and structural trust.

Think about teammates you've had with whom you've disagreed professionally, or who, because of their position, have impeded or stymied what you were trying to achieve. When we're able to sit down with the other person and address these challenges solely because of the strong personal trust in our relationship, we can often repair that breakdown in trust and reach a mutually agreeable solution. If so, it is due to your mutual respect, caring, and commitment. This is why we put such an emphasis on building personal trust in working relationships.

rule six

PRAISE AND CELEBRATE

Recognition is essential to FedEx culture—it's the bedrock on which the company's global brand and reputation is built. No matter where you are in the world, if you respect your people and you reward and recognize the right behaviors, they will deliver exceptional performance. That may sound like fluff, but it's a hard-nosed business approach. The difference between our team members doing their best and doing the minimum is the difference between success and failure. It directly affects our bottom line.

RAJ SUBRAMANIAM, president and COO, FedEx

I n 2010, as General Motors was emerging from bankruptcy reorganization, the leadership of the company's North America division recognized that reviving its fortunes depended on improving the customer experience at GM's thousands of independent franchise dealerships. In order to achieve that, GM introduced a new program called Trusted Advisor for the district managers heading the GM field sales team.

The objective of Trusted Advisor was to transform the district manager role into more of a strategic partner for car dealers, someone who could help dealerships grow their business and meet sales goals while also enhancing the customer experience. In other words, Trusted Advisor's goal was to establish a co-elevating co-creating relationship between every GM district manager and every dealership franchise in its vast North America network.

But Mark Reuss, GM's president of North America, didn't try to turn the tide for thousands of dealerships all at once. Instead, he and his executive team started small, with just fifty district managers, each of whom concentrated on one dealer. The idea was to evolve this new way of partnering on a small scale and to get it right before evangelizing their successes to their peers.

Mark recognized that the best way to raise the morale of his sales staff in the aftermath of bankruptcy was to create a winning momentum. As soon as the new Trusted Advisor program started showing glimmers of success, he and his team began praising and celebrating their progress.

It didn't take long. Within the first few months, good news stories started coming in as the Trusted Advisor district managers began helping their dealers improve profitability in their leasing rates, parts sales, and automotive sales. New ideas were tested, such as offering new model loaner cars to service customers whose leases were coming due.

As Mark and his team examined these early results with our team at FG, we evaluated each new practice carefully to confirm that it was innovative, achieved measurable outcomes, improved the customer experience, and was replicable. Once we landed on the best new practices reported from the field, Mark sent all kinds of generous shout-outs to the district managers and their dealer partners for their ingenuity and commitment. The specifics of each new practice were included in Mark's weekly communication sent out to the entire field sales force, so they could be easily tried and adopted.

Mark's personal commitment and passion made all the difference. He was always quick to pick up the phone and personally call to praise whichever district manager had most recently reported having co-created a new productive approach with his dealer. Mark even went out and adopted one dealership himself, so he could get a hands-on sense of the new practices and see for himself how they worked. As a leader, Mark personified going higher together and set a tremendous example that was recognized by his entire field sales team.

From the very first year of the program, astounding stories of success poured in from those fifty Trusted Advisor dealerships. Parts sales in one dealership rose more than 44 percent. Another dealership's leasing rate went from near zero to 45 percent, and monthly sales climbed 41 percent.

Soon, Mark's entire executive team was running a national campaign of praise and celebration for all these local success stories and the co-elevating partnerships behind each story. They produced videos of model practices that went out weekly, along with write-ups of the astounding results put through all of GM's internal and franchise communications. Dealers were invited to GM's regional and national events, where they were celebrated and, in turn, where they sang the praises of GM and its new Trusted Advisor partnership model.

By personally praising these early small wins at the dealership level and then celebrating their success far and wide, Mark and his team ignited a movement within the GM North America sales division. Sales managers and dealerships alike began clamoring for the changes that had produced such extraordinary rises in revenue, market share, and customer satisfaction. The Trusted Advisor program, through co-elevating co-creation between dealers and district managers, created a new model for customer service and profitability at GM's franchise dealerships, generating momentum for GM's turnaround organizational transformation.

LIKE RAYS OF SUNLIGHT

The GM story shows how small amounts of focused, positive energy can create exponential benefits throughout an organization. Whenever we lead without authority, serving our teammates as their champion and cheerleader is one of our highest-leverage responsibilities. Praise and celebration are key complements to caring and accountability, and accelerants to opening porosity as well. When we offer praise and celebration to someone today, it will make our next difficult day together that much more manageable.

My friend Philippe is the head of a global advertising agency whose clients include some of the biggest Fortune 500 companies. Whenever I'm with Philippe, he spends a lot of his time on the phone. Usually, I'm the guy juggling two phones at once, punching out texts on one while on a conference call on the other. But Philippe has me beat by miles.

"How do you get anything done if you're always on the phone?" I once asked him, equal parts kidding and curious. He looked up from his phone, grinning.

"This is the simplest and best tool ever invented for client-and-colleague engagement and satisfaction," he told me, holding up his phone. "This is the most important part of my job. No matter how many meetings I have, or how long my to-do list, I always honor my encouraging-word ritual."

Philippe's "encouraging-word ritual" involves calling, texting, or emailing an ever-rotating list of nearly one hundred clients and associates, offering them a regular stream of cheerful words of praise and celebration.

As Philippe sees it, he's giving his team and his clients much-needed encouragement and support in a disrupted and uncertain world. "It's so important to keep energy levels high and to keep everyone's momentum going strong," Philippe said. His associates have a tough enough job reimagining and relaunching their clients' brands against newer, bigger, and better competitors. "It's so much for people to shoulder, that I have one primary job: to keep the energy and movement up, up, up.

"We're asking clients to totally rethink their go-to-market strategies," he said. "Everyone is so focused on what's going wrong and needs fixing and how they need to do more, work faster and better, and whether any of their ever-increasing advertising spending will pay out. They work mad hours in highly stressful environments with intense pressure."

Philippe has an encyclopedic knowledge of his clients' work, and their personal lives, too. Sometimes he'll dig around on social media to find something special to celebrate—a trip they just took, a birthday celebrated, or some positive bit of company news. He really works at it, but he makes sure his encouraging words are always authentic. "I'm genuinely happy and excited to celebrate people's successes," he said. Calling his clients and colleagues all day gives him real joy and has the benefit of keeping his own spirits high.

Philippe's daily encouragement rituals remind me a lot of Seano, my personal coach. On any given day, out of the blue, he'll call, email, or text me with words of praise and celebration. He calls it "loving up" on people.

A typical voice text from Seano might read, "Keith, my brother. Wanted to send you some love and tell you how much I dug your TED Talk on co-elevation. You are making a huge difference in the world. I also saw you are traveling like a crazy man. However you might be feeling, don't ever forget that you are making a difference." If I'm in the middle of a tough day or stuck at the airport between flights, Seano is like my emotional chiropractor, giving me just the mood adjustment I need.

Whenever we celebrate and praise our teammates, it's as though we're shining sunlight straight into their souls. That's been my experience, and it's backed by psychologists who have studied motivation and organizational behavior. Psychologist Dan Ariely, bestselling author of *Predictably Irrational*, found that praise is more highly valued than money. His research shows that even occasional compliments can be more impactful than cash bonuses when it comes to raising worker productivity and motivation.[1]

Researchers in another study found that when practicing physicians were offered and experienced positive affect—a pleasant feeling or a good mood—they improved their performance in problem-solving, decision-making, and cognitive organization.[2]

Physicians primed to feel good (even with the simple gift of a small package of candy) showed more flexible thinking and made accurate diagnoses more quickly than those primed in other ways, or those not primed at all.[3] The researchers concluded that positive affect fosters openness to ideas, flexibility, and creative problem-solving.[4]

I've recognized the importance of positive reinforcement for a long time, and I celebrated its benefits in my first book, *Never Eat Alone*. That's why I felt my stomach sink as Philippe went on about his "encouraging-word ritual." I realized I had fallen off severely in praising my own circle of contacts. Over the years, I had dropped my former habit of calling and singing "Happy Birthday" to the people whose birthdays popped up in my daily calendar. Ugh, I had work to do.

A few years ago, during a dinner with friends, I was seated across from Luke, a relatively new acquaintance who had recently sold his first company—a tremendous accomplishment for any entrepreneur. I congratulated him for growing his company and developing a product that had caught the eye of a major software company.

"Kudos to you, man," I told him. "What you've done in the last eight years, people only dream about." As I poured on the praise for his persistence, determination, and ingenuity, out of the corner of my eye I saw my friend Tony leaning into Luke's space. He crowded himself comically close to Luke until he was practically sharing his chair. I laughed and asked him what the heck he was doing.

"I just wanted to experience what it felt like to receive your praise," Tony said. We all got a big laugh out of Tony's joke at my expense. And it *was* funny—but not really. As a dear friend, Tony's always gotten heaping helpings of my caring candor and direct coaching. I often cut quick to the critical as a coach because I want everyone to achieve their fullest potential. I see it as an exciting opportunity for growth. But I had been stingy with my praise for Tony, and Tony found a humorous way to let me know how much he longed to hear more of it. So, thank you, Tony. That's a moment I won't soon forget.

In any relationship—professional or personal—you never know how your seemingly small words of praise and celebration might inspire a pivotal moment in someone's life. Michael Lewis, author of nonfiction bestsellers such as *The Blind Side* and *Moneyball,* told an interviewer in 2005 how Coach Fitz, his high school baseball coach, had changed how Lewis felt about himself just by expressing his confidence in him.

When Coach Fitz put Lewis into a game as a pitcher, with runners in a scoring position, he told Lewis, "There's no one I'd rather have in this position than you." Lewis believed him. He picked off a runner on third and struck out the next batter to end the inning.

As Lewis explained, Coach Fitz's real genius kicked in *after* the game. "He would create these very dramatic moments on the ball field and make them feel so important," said Lewis. "And when they worked out well, he would seize on them as the sort of defining moment of your character. After the game, he handed me the ball, and told the whole team that I was this person—and this was a completely implausible description of me—that I was this person who was good in the clutch, and that in pressure situations, that's who he wanted to have the ball. And this is sheer invention. But I tried to become that person. And from then on, my behavior changed in every way. I started to take the classroom seriously."

Coach Fitz went to the headmaster at Lewis's school and told him that Lewis's performance that day was an achievement he could build on. The headmaster called Lewis into his office and told him, "We're expecting more of you, you know. Billy Fitzgerald speaks well of you."

As Lewis tells it, "You don't think of such trivial moments being turning points in lives, but I actually regard that moment as a turning point, and that man orchestrated it."[5] Coach Fitz took a seemingly ordinary, mundane moment and transformed it into something heroic and meaningful. It took him maybe ten minutes or so to create an experience that Michael Lewis would never forget. Taking those ten minutes here and there is something all of us can do, at any time we choose, for our teammates and for everyone else in our lives. This is one of the great privileges of being a leader. It's a gift we share all too rarely.

RULE SIX: THE PRACTICES

If you want to strengthen your relationships and really open more porosity with teammates all around you, try being the biggest cheerleader for the people you know and care about. Take some time each day to set aside your critical thinking, even for a few minutes, and acknowledge their friendship, their spirit, their hard work, and their significance in your life. People are thirsting for this kind of acknowledgment.

And when you offer praise and celebration, notice how it makes you feel. Your own spirits will lift. When you're in a funk, you may find the best way out is by sending along a few notes of praise and thanks. I think of Philippe and Seano and I wonder, are they celebrators because they are naturally joyous people, or are they joyous *because* they're celebrators?

Watch how praising and celebrating others can strengthen your bonds with your teammates. Pretty soon, it becomes habit-forming. Here are some suggestions I've found useful in getting started.

Make It Personal, in Real Time

As soon as you see someone on your team do something well—big or small—acknowledge it. Any praise is better than no praise. Whenever possible, tie the praise to a specific action or behavior.

If you catch a colleague doing something right, acknowledge the action, and be sure to tell them how they made you feel, as well. When Shannon in my office sends me a follow-up email that repeats back my comments from our phone conversation, I let her know how much I appreciate it. I tell her, "Shannon, when you do that, I feel I can trust that we're not letting any balls drop. I really appreciate that. Thank you."

Jalen, the "director of people" at one of Silicon Valley's biggest start-ups, relies on this kind of specific immediate positive feedback in most of what he does. It's all about reinforcing positive behavior, he says. "Often, people don't realize what they're doing well," he told me. "If we shy away from telling them where and how they're excelling, then how will they know to continue the good stuff?"

At the end of one informal team meeting, I saw Jalen request everyone's attention and then take a moment to praise the way the meeting leader—who ranks several levels below him—had taken feedback, given feedback, and asked questions throughout the spirited exchange of ideas. "I think that's worth a quick note for us all," he said. "It's how we need to handle similar situations in the future, when each of us may be challenged in order to get to the best, most audacious answers."

Remember the Platinum Rule

Let me repeat the Platinum Rule: Do unto others *only* as they would like to be done unto. Public praise is great, but not everyone is comfortable with it. So know your teammates, and praise and celebrate them the way you know *they* would appreciate it the most.

So much of the power and effectiveness of praise comes from people feeling seen and acknowledged. But there are introverts in every workplace who would feel painfully embarrassed if you were to ballyhoo their accomplishments at an open meeting. Be considerate and realize that what they'd appreciate most is a handwritten note or a deeply appreciative email. When you deliver the praise in a manner that makes them feel most comfortable, they'll know you *truly* appreciate them for who they are.

There are other instances when private praise is just the right touch. I've sometimes called the parents of my associates just to acknowledge them and thank them for raising such an amazing individual. I once called the father of an associate named Frank and left a voicemail telling him what a great year Frank had had, and how proud he should be of his son. Frank told me years later that his father kept the message on his machine for the rest of his life.

Don't Be Afraid to Praise Imperfection

Our teams won't improve if we don't let them see a sliver of light they can walk toward during dark times. When your teams are on missions that are particularly tough or when they're having difficult moments, that's exactly when we need to praise them, even if the performance is not perfect and the results are not optimal. There's a saying that if you're going through hell, you have to *keep going.* Celebration and praise provide the fuel that restores and sustains us, helping us to keep moving forward through stretches of extreme difficulty.

For months I worked with Marty, a CEO who wanted to fire Jasmine, his head of strategy. Marty felt Jasmine was unresponsive to his needs and moved too slowly. He wanted firm answers yesterday, while Jasmine preferred gathering complete market data before drawing any conclusions. Many tried to help Marty see how Jasmine was a counterbalance to his shoot-from-the-hip leadership style. In several instances, Jasmine's deep analysis had prevented Marty from making serious mistakes that could have drained the company's earnings, although Marty never acknowledged her for it.

Finally, I told him, with some exasperation, "Stop the torture. Either start celebrating her wins and give her a shot at turning your impression of her around, or let her go." I wanted him to admit that he was just indulging his need to be right. If he sincerely wanted to improve Jasmine's performance, he'd have to start praising her when she did things right.

Marty agreed to try an experiment. Instead of criticizing what he didn't like, he began to acknowledge all the things Jasmine did that he viewed as serving the company mission. He began to compliment her on even the smallest improvements in the areas where he was still dissatisfied. I was glad to see him, after one meeting, go out of his way to compliment Jasmine for having great instincts and for trusting them. It took him a while to recognize that withholding praise from a struggling employee only leads to their performance deteriorating further.

In the grand scheme of things, validating others costs you nothing, while it offers the potential for exponential returns on engagement, productivity, and motivation, as well as the opportunity to build stronger bonds of loyalty and trust.

Younger workers often voice a desire to find meaning and purpose at work. Given that, it's particularly important to recognize their successes, to reassure them that their contributions make a difference. Doing so can be essential if you want to retain your top talent. A global study found that 79 percent of people who quit their jobs cited "lack of appreciation" as their reason for leaving.[6] Millennials, in particular, are proving to have a much lower tolerance than past generations for negative work environments and work cultures that lack in acknowledgment. They want to be recognized for their efforts, for showing up and applying themselves, for keeping in the game. If your company can't recognize their contributions, they'll seek employers who do.

I've heard old-school managers mock younger employees for being this way. My response? Get over it. If celebration and praise is the fuel that restores and sustains us, then give everyone a damn medal. Millennials are the largest generation in today's workforce, so it's a lot less expensive to pass out compliments, medals, and ribbons than to absorb the costly turnover when all your top talent abandons ship. And frankly, the desire for recognition among millennials lifts all boats. The old-school managers might not want to admit it, but most of their older employees would also love to receive a hearty pat on the back now and again. It's likely that they gave up expecting any acknowledgment a long time ago.

Our need for positive reinforcement is truly universal. It even transcends species. At FG, where our research team ventures far and wide to report back practical ideas, I once had the opportunity to interview one of the trainers who appeared in *Blackfish*, the documentary about killer whales at SeaWorld. He said that to train an orca, you must use *positive* reinforcement almost exclusively. "If you use the stick too much," he said, "they'll kill you."

> We're a results-oriented, high-performance company that wins by creating value for our customers. It's important to take the time to celebrate those wins and acknowledge our teammates' contributions. That's how we keep co-elevating and flying in formation, all moving forward as one.
>
> TONY BATES, CEO, Genesys

Celebrate the Momentum of Winning

By recognizing even small victories, we show the way to larger, more sustainable achievements. The GM example illustrates the value of celebrating the *momentum of winning*. GM generated enormous enthusiasm for its shift to the Trusted Advisor model by celebrating small wins, one co-elevating partnership at a time. Then, as those Trusted Advisors and dealers copied each other's best practices, the results for the dealerships continued to mount. From there the contagion effect ensured that Trusted Advisor would catch fire as a movement.

If the Trusted Advisor program had been launched nationwide all at once as a top-down baked-and-shipped solution, its results would likely have been more mixed and diffused. The small initial group of fifty Trusted Advisor dealerships never would have gotten the focused attention they needed to become laboratories for innovation. And with no small-win momentum, the initiative would have run out of gas before its best practices ever had a chance to be developed and celebrated.

I didn't used to believe in small wins. I reserved praise and celebration for "big wins," like winning a mega account, having a CEO give us a shout-out for their share price increase, publishing a significant research study in *Harvard Business Review,* or having one of our books on the *New York Times* bestseller list. But these big wins don't happen every day. If that's all you ever celebrate, you're going to have a hard time keeping team spirit high.

Today I recognize that big wins are a by-product of stringing together lots of smaller wins along the way, and each of those wins deserves celebration. It's given me an entirely new arsenal to foster productivity throughout my life. I see how homing in on what our *team* is doing right is what exponentially boosts performance and productivity. We still identify and fix problems, of course; it's just not our sole focus. And when you celebrate people for doing things right, you'll find they're so much more energized and engaged in fixing what they've done wrong.

My younger foster son had such a troubled record at school that seeking small wins proved to be a lifeline for us. When he first came to us, he was disrespectful, disruptive, and disobedient in almost every way you can imagine. At school, he was totally checked out. I put him in a private Catholic school, and he was thrown out. Then I got him into a specialized private school, and the same scenario started to unfold again.

I wanted to fix everything for him, but I couldn't. At some point, I realized I just needed to get a win on the table for my boy. If he could just see himself as a winner, take pride in something, maybe that would prove to be a tipping point, where he'd develop a desire for another small win, and then another.

One afternoon, I was driving him and some of his buddies home from the movies, when I heard the guys freestyle rapping in the back seat. That was the first time I'd ever heard him rap. He was good. Damn good. The next day, I tried to make a big deal out of his rapping, upping the positive encouragement. He brushed aside my comments, saying he was just messing around.

"Well, I think you're pretty darn good, and I'm excited for you," I told him. "You were hands down the best freestyle rapper last night." He didn't say much after that, and I left our conversation on a positive note. The next time he and his friends were in the back seat, I hit record on my phone. When we got back to the house, I said, "Listen to this. I want you to hear how good you are." As he listened to it, he leaned closer to my phone and started to smile.

My kid didn't smile much at the time. That momentary glimmer of pride on his face, however fleeting, felt like a breakthrough.

We messed around with the recording, making edits and re-recording for almost an hour. He was grinning, and although he probably wouldn't admit it, he was looking for my encouragement and feedback. And I was so excited to give it to him. After our impromptu jam session, I nonchalantly said we could get him a rap coach if it was something he wanted. He agreed, and I wasted no time getting friends in the music business to help me track down a young artist who was starting out who had volunteered to work with kids. Ultimately, he and I even collaborated on an initiative we called Words to Life, within our Greenlight Giving foundation, that would help other foster kids tell their stories with pride, not shame, through the medium of rap music.

Much of my son's world at the time was pretty crappy, but here was one area where he flourished and that we could celebrate together. His self-esteem grew and our relationship improved as I continued to encourage him and give him positive reinforcement. That allowed for a pause in my role as the nag, disciplinarian, and authority figure. Once we were no longer locked in constant combat, I could feel my relationship with him grow as I watched him come alive with his music.

I approached his English teacher at school and asked if he could work on spoken word poetry instead of the other assignments where he was falling behind. His interest in school improved, and a couple of semesters later he made the honor roll. We had just needed to find one area for him to start winning in, and for me to highlight the momentum he was building so it could cascade into other areas in his life.

At LHH, our team coaching approach focuses on recognizing and developing the unique talents and working styles of the group to improve the quality and productivity of the team. If we want our teams to be motivated and proactive in getting things done, we have to seek out the opportunities to praise and celebrate their positive behaviors whenever we can. When we publicly laud our workers' contributions and achievements, we inevitably build a greater sense of purpose on our teams, and foster closer connections among teammates.

RANJIT DE SOUSA, president, LHH

Build Your Brand as a Celebrator

My friend Roy is a successful biotechnologist and entrepreneur, and someone I think of as my emotional uncle. I've never heard him say a bad or critical thing about another person. Everything he says is always positive and caring.

When Roy makes introductions, he always heaps out-of-this-world praise on the people he's introducing. I've heard him praise me as "brilliant, the inventor of behavioral engineering that has turned around the biggest companies in the world, and one of the top people who will absolutely change your life." Over the top, to say the least.

It's a little embarrassing, but Roy does this with everyone. His personal brand is intimately tied to his infectious habit of effusively celebrating others. And it makes him someone people enjoy being around, and naturally trust, even if his enthusiasm makes him prone to occasional exaggerations.

I've tried to adopt some of Roy's style as I've worked to build my own brand as a celebrator. In the workplace at FG, I'm embarrassed to admit how hard it is for me to remember to switch off the drive and constant focus on us doing more toward our mission, and the critical appraisal in my head that's always measuring what *hasn't* been executed as well as it could have been, and where might we possibly fall short.

A lot of this comes from my upbringing. My parents instilled in me this drive to perform and become the best, so I could live a better life than they had. They pushed me hard because they wanted so much more for me. As a result, whenever I fell short of any obvious marker of success, I was very hard on myself. I was worried I had disappointed them, and that I would fail to fulfill their heartfelt expectations in me.

That experience gave me a lifetime of mental habits that served me well early on but that I've had to undo as a leader. I take our mission at FG extremely seriously, so I tend to obsess over mistakes. I see ways people can improve and areas where they can grow, and I've never been shy about letting them know. And when someone accepted my advice but didn't adapt as fast as I believed they could, I made that clear, too. In every case, I believed my critique was of the utmost service to them, but my feedback hasn't always been taken that way.

Criticism is only *half* the job of coaching. The other half is celebration. When you celebrate your teammates publicly, it builds your brand as a co-elevator and serves your mission by attracting others to join with you.

Try sending a text to five team members who have come through for your shared mission recently, whether it's a short-term project or a longer-term goal. Tell them you were just thinking of them, and that you wanted them to know how grateful you are for their partnership. There's no need to lay it on too thick. Be authentic. Stay real. Tell them how you truly feel. Then watch how they respond.

Take an Unreasonable Stand

Some people need us to believe in their capabilities more than they're willing or able to believe in themselves. We need to champion these people, who, for whatever reason, aren't great at championing themselves. A friend of mine calls this "taking an unreasonable stand" for the other person.

Coaching teams to change their behaviors is often an uphill slog. Most people really don't believe it's possible for individuals to change, let alone undergo *transformative* change. They concede that *maybe* they can influence a handful of people, but at scale, for hundreds or thousands? No way! They can't see how it's possible to transform the values, principles, and attitudes that have created their workplace culture.

The unreasonable stand I take in these instances is to remind them they are no strangers to change and transformation. I challenge them to recall successful change initiatives they've been a part of in the past. The older employees respond with stories about Six Sigma, the quality movement of the 1980s, or, more recently, the transformation of workplace safety standards. They admit that those changes didn't seem possible at first. They'll recount how the changes transformed their work, and how they became the new normal after years of hard work and diligence. I sometimes remind them of our smoking laws; thirty years ago, people smoked in trains, the smoking sections of planes, restaurants, and at work. Few people then could have foreseen how completely we were able to change smoking culture.

Other times, I'll ask executives to tell me about the highest-performing team they have ever been blessed to be a part of. "What behaviors did your team exhibit? What was the biggest challenge you had to overcome? What did you do to overcome it?" That prompts them to recall their own experiences of resilience and perseverance. They remember whatever it took for them to win—perhaps it meant collaborating with someone they didn't get along with, making fast unexpected pivots in surprising directions, or leading the team into uncharted territory.

What these people need to do, what we all need to do, is recognize what we've overcome in the past and celebrate it, with an eye toward what we can achieve next. Take your past victories and project them into the future. By recognizing and celebrating what you've achieved, you can open the door to possibility. Next, share this spirit of hope with your teammates. Celebrate their achievements and successes when they're feeling down or lost or overwhelmed. You'll not only help boost their performance in the short term, you'll help them feel more motivated and inspired to take on the next big challenge they feel might be beyond their grasp.

This is how I convinced Liam, a former colleague at FG, to fully engage on a project with several new clients. Liam had been the project lead on our largest account at a celebrated industrial turnaround. But as that job wound down, he balked at his next assignments. He told me that after his previous success with that big client, he realized there was a greater risk of failure in juggling multiple accounts with new clients in industries he wasn't familiar with. He wanted to know, "What if they fail? Will I still have a job?" I was asking him to take a big jump, and he was feeling insecure.

Had I simply assigned Liam to these new accounts, without doing anything more, I believe it would have doomed him to failure. Instead, I wanted him fully invested in his new role, to feel engaged and excited by it. "Everything you want is within reach," I assured him. "You just have to take a step toward it." The only way I could elicit his best performance and commitment was to take a stand he felt was unreasonable and help him to connect the dots between his past success and where he wanted to go.

Three dinners and a lot of encouragement later, Liam embraced the opportunity, and then he knocked it out of the park. He led multiple teams in teaching FG techniques and tactics to large sales organizations, helping those companies grow their sales pipelines by billions of dollars.

Hope, which is defined as "the belief that things could be better and that you can make them better," may account for as much as 14 percent of productivity in the workplace.[7] There is no greater gift you can give someone than the gift of hope. By helping them to see themselves and their abilities with fresh eyes, you remind them they are fully up to facing any challenge before them.

After my sister, Karen, passed away from cancer, I grew concerned that my mother might shut herself up in her Pittsburgh home. She started complaining that she was having trouble walking and that perhaps she would forgo the annual trip to Florida for the winter that I would give her for the holidays, a retreat from Pittsburgh's cold that she had enjoyed so much in the past.

I took an unreasonable stand for my mother and her mobility. I told her I wanted her to enjoy Florida, and I promised to take her on an Alaskan cruise with me if she could work on her physical strength. I hired a trainer to visit my mother's house twice a week, and within a few weeks, they were sending me videos of the progress my mom was making. I posted the videos on Instagram so her friends could celebrate her achievements and share in her success and revived sense of hope. The unreasonable stand worked, and we're scheduling that Alaskan cruise.

> In my decades as a founder and CEO, I have almost instinctively used many of the principles of co-elevation, particularly the principle of praise and celebration. I've found that thanking someone for a job well done on Twitter and Instagram creates a flywheel of goodwill. Team members get a thrill from being praised so publicly, while social media followers feel more positively toward our company when they see the deep well of gratitude I have toward my team.
>
> SPENCER RASCOFF, former CEO, Zillow Group

Remember Gratitude

There is always something to celebrate if you look for it. On a tough day, or whenever you might find yourself feeling little cause for celebration, try tapping into your sense of gratitude. Make it a habit to ask yourself, "What am I grateful for today? What do I appreciate about my teammates, my clients, or my job?"

Paying attention to what you feel grateful for has the benefit of putting you in a positive frame of mind. Studies show the benefits of gratitude extend well beyond what we imagine, from improving our health, happiness, and relationships to boosting our alertness, determination, and self-esteem.[8]

In addition, expressing your gratitude extends all these positive benefits to others. A quick note of gratitude can be as simple as, "Thank you for responding so quickly to my emails. Most people take hours, if not days, to reply. You make me feel like I really matter." And there's nothing easier than recalling a past favor with gratitude: "Something just reminded me of that day that you [fill in the blank]. That was so great of you to do that. I'll never forget it."

This gratitude prompt has helped me to better understand what I appreciate most about my teammates, even the ones who challenge me the most. I've realized how much I value my teammates' ability to listen without judgment, their loyalty, their respectful disagreement when we see things differently, and their ability to lighten the mood or to help me feel more upbeat and confident about the future. I also feel grateful for those people willing to challenge my ideas and to hold me accountable.

All day long, problems and complaints about things going wrong will find ways to demand your attention. If you can make an effort to step away from your problems for just a minute and dash off a note of gratitude or two, I believe you'll find yourself uplifted and with just a little more energy to go back and face the latest emergency.

Celebrate Mistakes and Failures

My friend Philippe continues his ritual of sending colleagues and clients daily words of encouragement, because so much of transformational work is difficult and discouraging. It's not enough to offer co-workers praise for their achievements and celebration on their special days. You must also praise and celebrate mistakes and, yes, even failures.

"Celebrate failure, not just success," former Coca-Cola Company chairman and CEO Muhtar Kent said in a 2018 speech. "If I would do anything different in my thirty-six years of career, then it would be to create an atmosphere which allows mistakes, as you learn so much from mistakes. We are not bold enough to take enough risks, and risk is critical for success. We don't make enough mistakes."[9]

Risk-taking and innovation are key to transformation. But some experts estimate that as much as 90 percent of innovative projects end in failure. "One of my jobs as the leader of Amazon is to encourage people to be bold," CEO Jeff Bezos said in 2014. "[But] it's incredibly hard to get people to take bold bets . . . [If] you're going to take bold bets, they're going to be experiments. And if they're experiments, you don't know ahead of time whether they're going to work. Experiments are by their very nature prone to failure. But a few big successes compensate for dozens and dozens of things that didn't work."[10]

Bezos sets the example by celebrating his company's failures. "I've made billions of dollars of failures at Amazon.com, literally billions of dollars of failures," he said. "But they don't matter. What really matters is that companies that don't continue to experiment, that don't embrace failure, eventually get in a desperate position where the only thing they can do is make a kind of Hail Mary bet at the end of their corporate existence."[11]

Even successful innovations are the beneficiaries of screwups and setbacks during their creation. The world's top-selling spray lubricant is called WD-40 because the inventor's first thirty-nine tries were failures.[12] With the celebration of failure embodied right in the company name, it's not surprising that the WD-40 company culture is strong on celebrating mistakes and setbacks.

"At WD-40 Company when things go wrong, we don't call them 'mistakes,'" the company's employees are told. "We call them learning moments. We applaud the opportunity to openly discuss, learn, rectify, grow from our learning moments and share with others to avoid repeated learning moments."[13]

Experts who have studied failure say that learning is the obvious benefit of celebrating failure, but only if the failure is honestly studied and discussed. A universally hailed learning model is the military's after-action review or postmortem, in which everyone meets to talk over what was expected, what happened, what went wrong, what went right, and why.

Ego, defensiveness, and finger-pointing all need to be set aside for an after-action review to work. Celebration acknowledges the audacity of trying something new, and can give teammates the psychological safety they need to be honest and open about how they performed. Celebration, rather than condemnation, gives participants the courage necessary to learn, and then go back and try again.

The other essential benefit of celebrating failure is that by removing the stigma of shame, you get a much clearer picture of what went wrong than if embarrassed teammates spin their mistakes or sweep them under the rug.

Wernher von Braun, father of the US space program, knew this well. Back in 1954, a failed rocket launch had left everyone on von Braun's team baffled about the cause. They had begun work on a suspect component when an engineer from prelaunch preparations stepped forward. He told von Braun he'd seen a spark while tightening a connection on the rocket engine before the launch, but had thought nothing of it and told no one. That turned out to be the source of the launch failure, saving von Braun's team hours of needless work on the other component. Von Braun celebrated the engineer's mistake and his honesty by sending him a bottle of champagne.

Said von Braun at the time, "Absolute honesty is something you simply cannot afford to dispense within a team effort as difficult as that of missile development."[14]

Von Braun's observation has relevance today in any industry you can name. In the midst of disruptive change, every transformative team effort faces the kinds of difficulties and uncertainties that were common in the space program in 1954. Every company has one or more "moonshot" projects under way, with people working long hours at the very edges of their talents and capabilities.

If we want our teammates to be proactive in getting things done, and, if we want them to inspire and motivate each other, then that is what we need to seek out, praise, and celebrate, whenever and wherever it occurs.

What we reward with praise is what others will aspire to achieve. What we celebrate is what we will receive.

CO-ELEVATE THE TRIBE

> To lead your team, you must remind each and every teammate that they are responsible for maximizing each other's capabilities. That means supporting each other's strengths and coaching each other on your weaknesses. The old model—the heroic leader taking command—was never very realistic, and now it's obsolete. The team must serve the team, and the leader's role is to facilitate that co-elevation.
>
> BOB CARRIGAN, CEO, Audible

A friend who works for a TV network called one day to discuss a serious personnel problem at one of the network's most successful shows. Top executives were debating whether to cancel the show because of complaints about the lead actor's behavior, which she described as "dismissive, domineering, and rude." The on-set dynamics were dysfunctional, good people were threatening to quit, and there were rumors of lawsuits. Despite the show's high ratings, she said, the network brass still might pull the plug.

"Would you be willing to coach the lead actor?" my friend asked. "I don't know if it would interest you, but there's a lot at stake here." She explained that the show's production season had recently ended, and that the renewal decision would be up in the air for the next several months.

I rarely do one-on-one coaching, because I believe it takes team coaching to create significant sustainable results. But team coaching wasn't possible in this case, because the show wasn't in production. Given those circumstances, I had an idea for a different approach. Perhaps I could encourage the lead actor to build an on-set co-elevating team that would coach her to change her behavior. If that worked, the team members could coach others on set, so the workplace becomes a tribe of co-elevators.

I agreed to have dinner with the actor, a woman I'll call AJ. My friend had cautioned me that AJ was "very intense and focused, very dedicated to her craft." Maybe that was the angle, I thought. Perhaps I could challenge AJ to channel some of her intensity and focus toward promoting a positive co-elevation culture on set.

A week later, I arrived at the restaurant in Brentwood a little early. But AJ was already waiting for me, seated at a table and reading a script. After we exchanged pleasantries, I was surprised to learn she had looked me up and was familiar with my work. Of all the referrals I've had over many years, no one had ever shown up better prepared for our initial meeting.

It became clear in our conversation that AJ was a proud perfectionist who had disdain for everyone who failed to live up to her personal sky-high standards. At the end of shooting days, when everyone else would go out to dinner, she stayed behind to work on the next day's lines. Socializing with the cast, she said, wasn't important to her. "I've been in this business for a long time," she explained. "The success of the show is directly related to the energy I put into it."

AJ said she had a specific artistic vision for her character and for what she wanted to create with the show. From her perspective, all the real problems on the set were caused by others: a costar who was frequently unprepared, the show's producers who cared more about budgets than quality, and the ungrateful network executives who failed to support her despite her enormous contributions to the show's long-running success.

AJ was right that as the lead, she defined the show. But leadership, in her case, needed to go beyond the quality of her acting. She had to

people who cared about the show and might be willing to help AJ improve not only her own behavior, but the entire work environment. As a start, I asked AJ to name the one person in the cast whom she trusted the most, ideally someone who could also connect with the rest of the cast and crew. I was hoping there was someone with whom AJ had already established psychological safety, someone to whom AJ would listen. This person needed to have the courage necessary to partner with AJ in changing her behavior toward others and give her candid feedback whenever her behavior slipped.

AJ quickly identified a young actor, Miguel, whom she liked and respected, and the three of us met a week later at that same Brentwood restaurant. I explained to them that their new jobs on set would be to serve as co-elevators, first with one another, and then with everyone else on the team.

But I didn't want them to feel like saving the show would be a chore, like digging out of a ditch. Instead, I helped them find their shared mission. I set a North Star for them, a powerful and audacious goal to create an on-set culture like no other in their industry. It would be a set where everyone supported each other, one where everyone experienced more professional and personal growth than they had in any other project they had been a part of. It would be an on-set culture for the Hollywood history books.

As AJ and Miguel considered this possibility, both started singling out members of the cast and crew they were certain wouldn't go along with the idea. They even speculated how certain cast and crew members would try to undermine it.

"Look, you are going to meet resistance," I told them. "I don't give a damn about the people who won't go along." All that mattered at the start, I explained, was that they identify a small core group that *could* be on board, and start co-elevating with them. "Before you start worrying about what's not possible, let's talk about who might be your next partner." I asked if they could think of anyone who was open-minded, patient, and ready to step up and help save the show.

Miguel mentioned Wendy, a producer with whom he had a strong relationship, and the four of us met for dinner the following week. It would be up to this core group of three to lead the culture change on the set.

In advance of the dinner, I had asked AJ to stifle any negative talk that might arise and to ask Miguel and Wendy to focus instead only on the shared mission. During the dinner, things went well for about a half hour, until Wendy started singling out crew members she felt were likely to thwart their efforts.

"Okay, we need some ground rules," AJ said. She began a kind of recontracting conversation, setting out the boundaries for their collaboration. "This isn't about the others. Not yet. This is about us. This is about *our* commitment to the show and *our* integrity as leaders. How we show up on set and how we behave on the set will determine what the others make of this. Our behavior and our efforts to invite them to join us will determine whether they get on board or not. So let's keep the subject on ourselves."

I couldn't have said it any better. Any change starts by exploring opportunities, not by looking for obstacles and sowing division. I suggested they make a pact that they would never talk behind the back of any other member of the cast or crew *unless* the intention of the discussion was to be of service to that person's growth, before going to that person directly afterward. If any problem arose on set, I asked them to swear off the habit of complaining and instead promise to have an empathetic conversation with the person best suited to address the problem.

Then I suggested they formalize a recontracting agreement with the guiding principles they promised to live by and share with others. Here's what they came up with:

1. We will forgive each other and not talk behind each other's backs.
2. We will suspend judgment and listen. When in dialogue with someone, we will actively seek to better understand them before speaking.
3. When someone shares their ideas, insights, or feelings, those ideas are acknowledged, respected, and heard.

4. We will commit to inclusiveness, and actively seek input from a broad set of cast and crew.

5. We will work in service of each other's growth as actors and entertainment professionals.

6. We will stay open to giving and receiving candid yet caring feedback.

This conversation proved to be a watershed moment for AJ, Miguel, and Wendy. In the weeks that followed, the three of them far exceeded my expectations. They enlisted two other crew members in their mission, and then added a few members of the cast. Each came to embrace their shared responsibility to create a more positive workplace.

Then, with AJ's personal assurance about her commitment to change, the network renewed the show for another season. The network's top brass was impressed by AJ's commitment, and by the fact that she had taken a leadership role with a core group of the show's cast and crew.

Months later, when the show returned to production for the new season, the on-set culture had undergone a radical shift. The infighting and bad feelings from the previous year's production season had vanished.

AJ went on to change her behavior in a way that transformed how others saw her, which in turn transformed the work dynamic on the set. Her reputation shifted quickly, and even the broader industry saw her in a new, more empathic light. No longer was she the feared prima donna, and the cast and crew no longer felt they needed to walk on eggshells around her.

Committing to these changes was all on AJ—but she didn't do it by herself. She had to enlist a team of co-elevators, and all of them became leaders without authority. They relied on each other for feedback to ensure that AJ and the group collectively didn't slip back into old behaviors.

Transformation on this level is a team sport, and we all have to play an active role in it. Ultimately, by helping to promote and instill a proactive, co-elevating mindset in each team member, our own burden gets lighter, as each individual initiates change with their peers, in pursuit of our collective goals, and in fulfillment of our shared mission.

> As a company with a rich and proud seventy-five-year history, our transformation to a digital solutions provider was no small feat. Co-elevation helped us redefine our leadership team so that individual members took mutual responsibility for their performance and development. By enhancing team members' accountability to each other, we were able to align our company culture with our vision.
>
> CHUCK HARRINGTON, CEO, Parsons Corporation

RULE SEVEN: THE PRACTICES

Whenever I have a big party at my house, I kick off the evening with a toast and a request for a favor. "As of now," I ask the guests, "could you all please become hosts with me?" I explain that with so many people, I'm afraid I can't be a truly attentive host for everyone. "If you see someone without a drink," I say, "please ask them if they want one. If you see someone standing alone, go up and chat with them. Introduce them to someone you know or invite them into your conversation. If we all take care of each other, we are going to have an amazing evening together."

Then I go so far as to ask everyone to acknowledge my request, which they always do loudly and with plenty of laughs. This is my active recontracting. At that point, I know I can relax and enjoy the party, certain that everyone will reach out to each other.

Leading without authority is a lot like hosting a big party. You're also devoted to being of service and making everyone feel welcome and at ease. And the best and easiest way to ensure that everyone is taken care of, without exception, is to explicitly enlist your teammates in taking care of each other.

As we gain momentum in co-creating and co-developing with colleagues, teammates, friends, and family, it's incumbent on us to enroll others in the same co-elevating mission. If we want to sustain the changes we're making as co-elevators, we need to support the spread of co-elevation beyond our own teams. Regardless of your formal title, the ultimate leadership achievement is to support and inspire your teammates to become leaders without authority in their own right. Then you can engage them in missions similar to AJ's, working with them to shift everyone's behavior throughout your workplace.

Here's how.

Turn Gossip into Gold

Negativity, whining, complaining, making yourself a victim—all are poison to co-elevation and any initiative for change. But expressions of pessimism can also provide great opportunities to be of service to our teammates through coaching: Whenever someone speaks disparagingly about a co-worker, flip the conversation so that the venting turns into positive action.

Recently one of my teammates at FG texted me, "Is Thomas no longer responsible for entering data in salesforce.com?"

"What do you mean?" I texted back.

"Well, he seems to be dropping the ball. Has he moved on to a different role, or gotten permission to skip the data entry?"

This teammate was making a veiled attempt to complain to the boss about a co-worker. It would have been so easy to be drawn in. I really had to fight the urge to text Thomas and question him. Then I stopped and realized I had a chance to reinforce our firm's commitment to co-elevation as our North Star by shifting the coaching to the team, for the team.

I texted: "The question I think you meant to ask me is: 'I'm worried that Thomas is stretched too thin to complete all his work. What I've noticed in particular is his lack of data entry. Do you have any insights about this and his priorities before I reach out to him and offer my support, or find out what we can do to help him get back on track?' "

Once I took a step back, I realized I didn't need to get involved at all. "You've got this. Just talk to Thomas," I continued. "Find out what's going on in his life. Find out if we need to renegotiate responsibilities as a team. Encourage him to come to the team on the next call, if that is the case. For the sake of our mission and Thomas's success, dive in and share responsibility for helping him figure this out. I'll be excited to hear how your outreach goes on next week's team call. In fact, why don't the two of you take a moment to report back to the team if you think that would benefit him and the team. Otherwise, I'll assume you two got things back on track."

The whole exchange filled me with excitement. Instead of indulging my habit of trying to fix it myself, I'd encouraged Thomas's teammate to adopt a co-elevating mindset and help Thomas solve his problem. That backhanded complaint about data entry became an occasion for two teammates to develop and grow and to seed a stronger co-elevation contract and culture.

Don't indulge in venting. And don't allow yourself to become a passive participant by ignoring it, either. Remember your responsibility as a leader to promote co-elevation among the team.

Talk Behind Your Teammates' Backs (but Only to Be of Service)

Whenever you have a problem with a teammate, I encourage you to sit down with that teammate in private and approach them about the problem in a supportive manner. However, before we make an approach, it sometimes makes sense to gather some insights by conferring with another teammate or two, but only with the intent to help out the person needing support: "I think Joshua is falling behind. How can we help him? And what's the best way to discuss this with him?"

In such cases, you don't want to get trapped in the snare of complaining behind someone's back. Be open and transparent about your sincere intentions. To me, these types of preparatory conversations are the *only* cases where it's okay to talk about teammates behind their backs, because it's an expression of your intention to elevate them. When we accept responsibility for the success of all members of our team, we are committed to helping them grow and develop and reach their full potential.

It's safe to assume that your teammate will find out that you have been soliciting advice from their colleagues. This shouldn't be a big deal if your intentions are pure. You'll have to decide how psychologically safe the person you are asking about might feel about all this. Be prepared to tell that person that you asked around first because you wanted to get all the facts, and that your aim is to build an even more successful relationship. Nothing needs to be done in the shadows, nor should it be.

In the early stages of working with clients, I begin with diagnostic interviews that help me understand their team's challenges, interpersonal dynamics, strengths, and weaknesses. I find that people are all too eager to share their frustrations about their peers and bosses. I hear from so many executives who are distraught and disappointed in their teammates' behavior. Venting our frustrations is natural, but unfortunately, it's often done in ways that are counterproductive and lack integrity.

Complaining about underperforming team members usually takes place in the shadows, in the form of griping to a colleague or the boss. Even worse, two colleagues will basically gossip about how a third one is not holding his own, without ever attempting to remedy the situation themselves. If we are honest, most of us have fallen into such behavior. But by so doing, we tend to absolve ourselves of any responsibility to support that team member and help them to elevate their performance. That is poor leadership.

Does blowing off steam actually help? No. It doesn't get you any closer to solving the problem at hand. It's akin to sitting on your back porch, nursing a Budweiser and kvetching about how you want to change jobs, without actually beginning a job search. It's empty talk with no action. It does nothing to serve the mission at hand.

Coach the Team Members Most at Risk

If a team member valuable to your mission is underperforming, causing trouble, or even at risk of getting fired, remember the ethos at West Point described on page 126: True leaders leave no one behind. Going higher together means *together*. Summon all your skills in serving, sharing, and caring, leverage the tribe for the tribe, and bring your maverick teammate back into the herd.

Simon was the chief data officer for a large family-owned transportation company in desperate need of a complete technology revamp to catch up with its competition. Unfortunately, despite the company's high hopes for Simon's ambitious modernization plan, his collaboration skills were so poor that he was soon at risk of being fired.

One day I received a last-ditch call from the head of HR, asking if I had any ideas for saving Simon from himself. Everyone knew that firing Simon would set back the tech revamp and damage the company, but they didn't feel they had a choice.

Simon's problem was that in a company that valued modesty and humility, he often went to such extremes to seek credit for his accomplishments that it cast doubt on his veracity. Simon needed the same behavioral support team that AJ had needed.

When I spoke to Simon, he put all the blame on the company's backward culture, and I didn't argue with him. Instead I told him that if he wanted to save his job, we needed to find a kind of interpreter for him to help him get in step with the company's culture. Simon was quick to identify Joshua, who ran supply chain operations for the company. When I met with Joshua, I got straight to the point. "You like Simon, right?" I asked. "Most people think he's not a fit for this company's culture. He's probably going to end up getting axed within a month or two. Are you up for helping him?"

Joshua believed that Simon was brilliant and somewhat misunderstood, but also recognized that he had some real issues to work on. What's more, Joshua's department needed Simon's technology insights very badly.

So Joshua was on board. My instruction for him was to coach Simon on how to collaborate with his peers. I suggested to him that Simon was just very insecure and needed his advice as to what to say and not say in meetings. I asked Joshua to give Simon a reassuring pep talk before every meeting in which they were both involved, and to give him some praise and caring coaching where appropriate afterward.

Joshua suggested that HR work with Simon on the mission as well, and he subsequently enlisted the department's help. Little by little, they enrolled others to help support Simon's development. Then the train really got rolling. People who respected each other but might have been dubious of Simon started helping each other help Simon. And Simon, in turn, began behaving better, to such a degree that even his biggest detractors noticed. Drawing on the power of celebration, I asked Joshua to make sure Simon's critics were aware of even the smallest new changes in his behavior.

Before long, Simon's improvement became a self-fulfilling prophecy: His boasting and other off-putting habits never completely stopped, but his behavior was no longer as egregious. Moreover, people saw this shift in him, and that he had been gaining supporters, and they started to see his value. Today his work is making a critical difference to the company's turnaround.

As in AJ's story, the organization's HR head played an important role in helping Simon's turnaround. I believe strongly that going forward, HR leaders will be important contributors to building a co-elevation movement in the workplace. The need for leading without authority is so great that we will need to work with HR to co-create ways of integrating co-elevation into traditional organizational design. In recent years, I've offered a co-elevation coaching series for HR heads from about sixty of the world's largest organizations. If you think your head of HR might be interested in learning more about this group, send me an email at kf@ferrazzigreenlight.com. Maybe your HR department can join this movement.

> Continuous transformation is the new normal in today's business world, and a co-elevation culture is what underpins the ability to gain and sustain velocity at great companies like Google and Ancestry. Co-elevation resonates deeply with what drives success at highly innovative companies, so we can rely more and more on other members of the team to support our mission and also each other. As co-elevation scales, it has the capacity to bring a richer sense of belonging to our workplace culture, and our lives. That's what nurtures the psychological safety needed to think big and pivot fast to take advantage of new insights and opportunities.
>
> MARGO GEORGIADIS, CEO, Ancestry

Keep Growing the Coaching Ranks

In developing your team, be creative in how you draw in the additional coaching resources you need to keep expanding the team's capabilities. Outside coaching has been vital in building my relationship with my younger foster son. There was a lot of cultural distance between us when we met. He was a twelve-year-old from the inner city, and I was in my forties, from rural Pennsylvania by way of Yale and Harvard Business School. We both grew up poor, but I'd had the benefit of consistent family support, and he hadn't. To reach him and help him develop, I needed reinforcements who had more porosity with him than I did. At first, it seemed like *everyone* had more porosity with him than I did.

I asked the social workers if they knew of any success stories of young men who had survived the system and were thriving beyond it. I wanted to find an eighteen-to-twenty-year-old who really had his life together after going through foster care, and was still young enough to relate to my son.

They introduced me to Victor, a nineteen-year-old former foster kid who was in a police academy training program. I hired Victor to serve as my interpreter and coach with my son. He'd hang out with us on weekends. He'd observe me with my son, and then advise me how to talk to him and when necessary discipline him, how to respond—or not—to his outbursts, and how to show him I loved him and that I wasn't going anywhere. He had plenty of time with my son to offer his own straight talk as well about my intentions and what my son's behavior could be putting at risk.

But I didn't stop there. I embraced my foster son's teachers and football coach and invited them to dinner at our home, just as my dad had invited my fifth-grade homeroom teacher to our house when I was being picked on at school because I was the scholarship kid in the class.

I wanted my son to have a maternal influence as well, from someone he could relate to, so I brought in Sunshine, a wonderful, warm, boisterous woman, originally from Barbados, as our household chef. We didn't need a chef, but I needed help raising my son. She had also been in foster care as a child and knew a lot about the perils of the system firsthand.

I also hired the rap coach mentioned previously in chapter six. We were determined to help my boy grow up confident and proud. I also enlisted my son's school friends, inviting them on our vacations and making our home a cool place where kids could hang out.

Through these co-elevating relationships, we had a team of people in my son's life to support him, guide him, and help him make choices and deal with his trust issues. My attempts to connect emotionally with him were supported by the voices and perspectives of others, all of whom were committed to his well-being and development. Expanding my team in these ways in service of his development was what it took for my son to begin co-elevating with this new tribe, so we could all get to a better place.

Create a Tipping Point

Maybe you already know who your first partners in co-elevation will be, or maybe you already have strong co-elevating relationships. I can't stress enough how important it is to open porosity with them and to serve, share, and care. You can build 10x results on the foundations of these first few strong co-elevating partnerships.

By the time I sat down with AJ to help save her TV show, I was confident it would take just a small co-elevating core group to spark a workplace-wide movement on their set. I'd seen it many times before, and our research at FG confirmed it. At GM, for example, we found that out of one thousand district sales team members, about two hundred accepted the challenge to adopt the new Trusted Advisor sales model, but only about fifty seriously took up the mantle.

That small, self-selected group of fifty spirited early-adopters made all the difference. They self-organized into small co-elevating teams, co-creating new solutions, supporting, coaching, and celebrating each other as they co-elevated with their dealer partners. They became a tight-knit community of evangelizing all-stars who produced outstanding sales results as they encouraged their peers to join them.

Participation in the Trusted Advisor program swelled. When roughly 30 percent of the division was participating, the movement hit a tipping point. Momentum and celebration of those winning teams became irresistible. So many salespeople had achieved outsize results and had become outspoken advocates for the new program that co-elevation became the new standard for sales behavior.

If you need a goal for building a workplace movement, those are pretty good numbers to use as guidelines. As you build your relationship action plans for each of your projects, take note of when you have co-elevating relationships with 5 percent of the names on your list. Enlist those team members in the effort to get around 30 percent into co-elevating relationships.

Just keep on inviting teammates to co-elevate, and before you know it, your workplace will have a whole tribe of people speaking the same language and leading without authority. Never give up on those who were part of the early resistance to change. Some may become what I call Saul-to-Paul converts. In the New Testament, Saul of Tarsus was an infamous persecutor of Christians until he was converted one day on the road to Damascus by a voice and a vision from heaven. He changed his name to Paul, joined the apostles, and went on to become the early church's greatest evangelist.

> We're leading the charge for what's never been done before, and that takes constant creativity and innovation from our small start-up team across a wide range of expertise—biology, chemistry, food technology, automation, and public outreach and education. So it's absolutely essential that we all come together as a team of "hands-on dreamers." Through co-elevation we're able to share our knowledge, pick each other up, and support each other in solving problems with no certain solutions.
>
> UMA VALETI, CEO, Memphis Meats

SPARKING A WORKPLACE MOVEMENT

Soon after AJ received word that the show had been renewed, I had a final meeting with AJ, Wendy, and Miguel as preparations began for production of the new season. I made a special request of Wendy and Miguel. "I need you both to commit to helping AJ and each other continue to develop and grow," I told them. "If AJ starts to get too intense, you've got to step in and help her hear other people's reactions and feedback, and make sure they feel valued, respected, and heard."

I reminded them that AJ would be starting this mission with very little goodwill on set. The three of them would need to visibly model the commitments they'd made to each other. They would have to keep adding new co-elevating members to the team, until everyone on set could feel that the environment had really shifted. And if at any point crew members or cast members started falling short of the contract they had made to each other—maybe blaming or finger-pointing—it would be up to them to control their emotions and invite different behaviors from their teammates with empathy and compassion.

"You not only need to coach one another and everybody else on the set," I said. "You're going to have to *love* on them. You're going to have to celebrate them and practice all the co-elevating principles we've worked on. You're the co-elevating coaches of the entire team. That's now your new job. Take it as seriously as you would preparing for an important new acting role."

I later learned that within weeks, the change in the show's on-set culture was noticeable. AJ, Miguel, and Wendy continued to add new members to their team. Eventually the team included many of the people AJ, Miguel, and Wendy had once pegged as likely obstacles to progress.

About a year later, I got a series of texts from one of the show's crew members, someone I'd never even met in person. He was one of the first people AJ, Miguel, and Wendy had enlisted after our dinner, back when the show's future still hung in the balance.

> From last year to this year there is an incredible difference in the energy here every day. I feel the camaraderie, the fellowship, the collaboration, but most of all the feeling that each and every one sincerely wants to help out the other.
>
> I told AJ about my son's incredible baseball coach. He tells the kids there's no team out there who can beat them if they come together as a team. That's how I feel our team is clicking. We're playing with our hearts onscreen and off.
>
> I would have never predicted this, but we keep growing closer. Everybody's really helping each other and wanting everyone to do well.

The show is still on the air in 2020, and since the culture shift, it has had some of its best ratings ever. Having once been under siege by the cast, crew, and network, AJ had become an authentic change agent, leading a movement to transform the show's on-set environment.

It's all on you to create a co-elevating team that achieves its mission and transforms your culture. Again, at the beginning, you have to do the heavy lifting. But when you are truly co-elevating and co-developing with your teammates, you'll inspire that behavior in others. Then it becomes everyone's responsibility to reach out, to co-create, to co-develop, and to ensure a level of co-elevation that says, "I won't let you fail."

The burden of responsibility becomes lighter when the mission is shared. That's how all of us go higher together. That's when we can each achieve 10x of our own capabilities and 10x on our goals. It's the tipping point where a team can spark a movement, and a movement can change a culture.

OLD WORK RULE: Co-workers who are uncooperative, difficult to work with, or not contributing are avoided and written off.

NEW WORK RULE: If one team member is holding back the mission in any way, the team gets to enlist the help of other teammates to elevate that team member and their contribution.

A CO-ELEVATING CONTRACT

Research has found that if we sign a contract obliging us to achieve our goals, we are much more likely to succeed at them.[1] That's what AJ and her team did when they recontracted their relationship with the shared mission of creating a new supportive environment on their TV production set. Here is a model recontracting agreement for any kind of co-elevating relationship.

1. **We are committed to the mission and to each other's success:** We will *not* let each other fail. In fact, we will ensure each other succeeds. We will elevate each other as we work together to achieve our shared mission.

2. **Collaboration:** We will collaborate, not sell each other on our ideas or bleed into consensus. We will be insatiably curious while breaking through to new levels of innovation. We will respectfully challenge the other's ideas and provide the candid feedback on the mission to attain better outcomes.

3. **Development:** We commit to helping each other develop our skill sets and/or behaviors so our performance improves. We give each other permission to trust our instincts and to give the candid feedback the other person needs to hear so we can grow.

4. **Speak truth:** We will speak the truth in service of the mission and each other. We give each other permission to trust our instincts and give feedback and candor when needed. We will see and receive such candor in service of each other because we care about each other's success.

5. **No victims:** Nothing will stand in the way of our transformation. We will divorce ourselves from the momentum of the past and will not accept any victim language. We will check each other if someone slips into a victim mindset and speaks like a victim.

6. **Look to ourselves first:** When feeling frustrated with the other person, we will look to change our own behavior first, asking, "What's my part?" before finger-pointing and blaming others.

7. **Spend the time to serve and care about the person:** We commit to serving and sharing with each other to deepen our relationship and building the psychological safety, so the other person knows we genuinely care about them.

8. **Celebrate:** We will celebrate and praise each other's performance and our wins.

JOIN THE MOVEMENT

> At Patagonia, we don't just have a culture, we have a movement. It's one of the most powerful differentiators a company can have when its people believe so deeply in shared values; and doing that, they not only practice this way inside the company but actively evangelize it in the world. And in our case our customers join us, co-activate with us, and lead as much as we do. We are a stoked co-elevating community; and that not only shows up in the conviction our employees and customers have to do more for our mission to save our home planet—but in our continued strong performance as well.
>
> DEAN CARTER, chief human resources officer, Patagonia

My highest purpose in writing *Leading Without Authority* is to help you incite a movement that will measurably enhance your life and the lives of those around you, while transforming the institutions that can alleviate suffering globally. The simple practices of this book have the power to bring about real cultural transformation, not only on your teams but throughout entire organizations you touch, and into the world at large.

I believe co-elevation will become a worldwide movement. It has to. The new work world demands it. With each passing day, as hierarchies are sapped of their influence, co-elevation grows in importance, expanding the ranks of leaders both with and without authority.

With time, I believe co-elevation will become a core human competency for living in an ever more diverse, fast-changing, and interdependent world. Co-elevation offers us all new routes to joy and personal growth—within our workplaces and beyond.

As our co-elevating habits transform our work relationships, they will naturally spill over into the rest of our lives. The co-elevation principles of broadly embracing diverse opinions with greater inclusivity, richer collaboration, elevated candor, and transparency in service of each other, mutual growth, and development can give us all new pathways to living our truth, in every dimension of our lives.

Change on this scale can be hard to imagine. But today's world was built by change movements of the past. Every movement begins when a small core of devoted believers feels a shift in the wind and sees a crumbling status quo. I'm reminded of that great quote attributed to the legendary anthropologist Margaret Mead: "Never doubt that a small group of thoughtful, committed citizens can change the world: indeed, it's the only thing that ever has."

That's the story of every great social movement, from civil rights to twelve-step recovery to any of the world's great religions. All of them sprouted from idealistic visions unlikely to change anything at all. But once people experienced the power of these new ideas, they spread the good news, movements took hold, and society at last absorbed those heady visions into what became the new normal.

I see a similar path for the co-elevation movement. Those of us who have experienced the magic of co-elevation will spread its message because the ethos of serve, share, and care makes co-elevation inherently contagious. People are generally slow to believe, but they are quick to adapt. When we reveal the tremendous value of co-elevation to our co-workers, when they witness its power to change behaviors, inspire teamwork, and produce unexpected outcomes, they will become believers.

I was raised in the Christian faith, and now I feel that co-elevation is how I want to bring my faith, my belief, to what it means to walk the planet as a good man, as someone who is humble, who gets stuff done, who leaves a footprint and a ripple effect when I'm gone. I want my children, my family, my community, and my workplace to have been positively affected because I chose to co-elevate with them.

So far, this book has focused on one person, you, changing your behaviors and elevating the people around you to greater success, mostly in the workplace. I hope you don't stop there. I hope you now go and teach co-elevation to others who then become part of this movement. Who's the next person leading their work who you're going to help ignite to be a member of our movement? Imagine if instead of hunkering down in our individual bunkers, pointing fingers and blaming other people, we paused and said, "Who do I need to start co-elevating with to achieve this mission or to solve this challenge?"

Make the biggest difference you possibly can. We spend so much time at work, why not have our co-elevating relationships there inspire us beyond the workplace, to co-create better relationships, better marriages, better families, and better communities?

I've described many of the occasions when I've used co-elevation to deepen my relationships with those I love and care about. People I've worked with tell me they find themselves using co-elevation language outside the workplace all the time. One HR executive introduced co-elevation to her women's executive group and the promise "to support each other through co-elevation" is now a part of the group's mission statement.

Another woman I know uses co-elevation as a guiding principle in her romantic life. "I realized I can't tolerate my most important relationships being anything less than co-elevating," she told me. "I want to elevate the people in my life, and honestly, I want them to want to elevate me, too. Anything short of that is unacceptable."

In 2019, I was invited to officiate two wedding ceremonies because both couples wanted the principles of co-elevation sanctified in their wedding vows. During the ceremonies, each couple celebrated their lifelong commitment to co-elevate by asking their gathered friends and family to hold them accountable and join them in going higher together.

I truly think of co-elevation in everything I do. It is the North Star I steer by, even when I find myself off course. At every talk I give, when I discuss co-elevation as the science of growing leadership and sales capabilities, I also strive to bring co-elevation right into the room. During the so-called networking breaks, I try to foster an environment of real co-elevating community.

My life mission is to bring about a world where we can walk into rooms full of strangers and the shared expectation is that we all skip the small talk and start the deep talk. We engage around serve, share, and care and all learn how to best be of service to each other and our respective transformational missions. I recall how after my father's passing, my mother's church grief group was particularly co-elevating for her, and so was her lifelong "card club girls" who met monthly not just to play cards but to support each other in the most powerful ways.

> The organization of the future will be defined by co-elevation and agility, with fluid, dynamic teams trailblazing and accelerating innovation. By broadening the definitions of "teams" and "leadership," co-elevation embraces the agile mindset necessary for success in a world that is increasingly more inclusive and radically interdependent. Every leader must embrace this mindset during a time when the way we all work and live is being redefined by disruption and digital transformation.
> PAT GELSINGER, CEO, VMware

I want to live in a world that respects the value of diversity enough to recognize that co-creation among a diverse set of perspectives will always yield the most powerful solution to every problem we face, where caring candor is a normal expectation, and where conflict avoidance, white lies, and polite fibs have no place in mutually respectful relationships. I truly believe that the everyday half-truths that people use to protect their fragile egos and positions of power will have no place in the radically interdependent and transparent world that's being born.

My dream is that this book will inspire new levels of thinking about co-elevation, enough to bring about cultural transformation in organizations throughout the world. Imagine schools, teachers, and parents using co-elevation to prepare children for a future in which co-creation is valued above all other workplace skills. Philanthropies and nonprofit organizations may need this cultural transformation the most, because their missions to help those in need are so urgent and vitally important that they can't afford to squander their resources through obsolete hierarchical thinking.

I offer my clients free coaching support for their philanthropic interests because I've seen its transformative effects. I've worked with the famous Summit Mountain Series to make co-elevation a foundation for its events, and I'm working with Tech T200, a group of top female chief information officers, to introduce co-elevation into the fabric of their contracts with each other. I'm also helping Peter Diamandis use co-elevation to take his XPRIZE Foundation and Abundance 360 organization to meet their huge and profound potential.

Personally, I've focused our Greenlight Giving foundation on a call for reform of the foster care system and saving the lives of the 150 million homeless and parentless children around the world. This focus has also led us to bring co-elevation to a national nonprofit dedicated to the prevention and treatment of child abuse. We've used co-elevation principles to enable its core group of donors to expand their ranks with a goal of 10x results in fund-raising growth.

At the World Bank Group, we launched a co-elevation movement among its regional branches, local governments, and other NGOs, all with the intention of leveraging billions into trillions of dollars in long-term financing toward the bank's audacious mission to eradicate global poverty. Through co-elevating team dinners, learning sessions, boot camps, and ongoing peer coaching, the World Bank Group expanded its commitment and capabilities, aiming at creating a 10x multiplier of the total funds it was able to deploy.

There are few institutions in more desperate need of co-elevation than government and the poisonous political culture that accompanies it around the world. Politicians rely on an "us vs. them" mindset to get elected, and then find they've built such thick walls around themselves that they are unable to govern. I've been in contact with US senators and other members of Congress to explore bipartisan opportunities to go higher together through shared commitments, despite their policy disagreements. I've also made myself personally available for coaching in places where civic conflicts and breakdowns signal the opportunity for a transformative co-elevating result.

Today's rising generation of political leaders face a daunting set of responsibilities in the coming years, responsibilities that can't possibly be addressed through divisiveness—problems like climate change, environmental degradation, population migration, bigotry, and genocide. I believe the co-elevation movement will open porosity between individuals with differing outlooks, so they can contribute powerful new co-created solutions to these problems, all of which are outgrowths of old, isolating, and destructive ways of thinking.

> Change in business is happening too fast to create breakthrough solutions relying on control and hierarchy to produce the innovation that we need to compete. Co-elevation is a path for team members to learn how to collaborate through authentic partnerships that allow the team to grow together, helping them keep pace with the extreme pressure of the marketplace.
>
> PAUL YANOVER, CEO, Fandango

My dream is that you and everyone who reads this book will bring co-elevation thinking to your local philanthropic and social commitments, and to your places of faith and worship. Now you can be deployed as a coach in your community where it matters most to you.

Your personal stories, told and celebrated, are fuel for this movement. As you apply this book to your life, please let me know about your outcomes, so that your example can inspire others. Has this book had a positive impact on you? If so, the greatest gift you can give me is to let me know your story. Send me a message at kf@ferrazzigreenlight.com and tell me how you've used co-elevation for greater productivity, creativity, and, most important, deeper relationships with the essential people in your life. With the help of the

FG team, we will co-create appropriate ways to share these stories more broadly and inspire others to go higher together.

This is just the beginning of a journey in which we are working to create a better world, one that can be more joyful and offer transformational outcomes beyond our wildest dreams. Through co-elevation, we will build our co-elevation movement.

FIRST TO WALK THE COURSE

When I was a teenager, my father got laid off from his factory job, and I took a job as a golf caddy at the local country club to help pay the family's bills. My father knew nothing about golf, but he gave me this advice: "Show up half an hour early each day."

I didn't understand his point, but I did it anyway. At first, I was bored stiff, waiting for the day to begin. But I then took the time early in the morning to walk the course. I tested the speed of the greens and began to notice little things. Which way the grass leaned after it had been mowed. How certain slopes were steeper than they appeared from the fairway. Where the tough pin placements were. By getting there early, one day after another, I developed a special feel for that course. I helped my golfers improve their scores, and I earned bigger tips. Other golfers started requesting me, and soon I was in demand. I won the club's annual caddy award, which gave me the privilege of caddying for golf legend Arnold Palmer that year at the club.

So that's my father's wise advice, a part of his legacy, which I'm now passing on to you. By reading this book, you've arrived at co-elevation early. Make the most of it. Keep this book handy and consult it often. Follow through on the practices and apply the new work rules to everything you do. You'll stumble from time to time, but your progress is what people will notice.

Now is your time to develop your own special feel for how to co-elevate and lead without authority. You'll develop your own unique insights about what works best with your teammates as you coach them, co-develop with them, and celebrate with them. In doing so, you'll contribute to the emerging movement.

And when that day finally arrives, when leading without authority and co-elevation are recognized as essential workplace skills, you'll be like the teenage golf caddy I once was. You'll have walked the course many times before, fully prepared for the challenges ahead.

acknowledgments

The practices, prescriptions, and evolving insights developed for this book owe so much to the thoughts and experiences of the hundreds of leading executives and their teams with whom we at Ferrazzi Greenlight have worked in recent years. It pains me to mention just one or two individuals for each account because so many contributed. I am grateful to all of them as my co-elevating partners. This book would not exist without them.

In chronological order of our project work, they include but are certainly not limited to: Lisa Buckingham at Lincoln Financial; Devin Wenig and John Reid-Dodick, both of whom I first met at Thomsen Reuters; Kristin Yetto at eBay; Mark Reuss at General Motors; Jack Domme and Scott Kelly at Hitachi Data Systems; Jim Norton at AOL; Stefan Beck of BASF and Robert Blackburn, who I first met there; Lisa Arthur at Teradata; Jeff Bell at LegalShield; Mike Clementi at Unilever; Tami Erwin, George Fischer, Diane Brown, Annette Lowther, Martha Delehanty, and Scott Lerner at Verizon; Jim Kim at the World Bank; Mike Dennison, who I first met at Flex; Chuck Harrington, Carrie Smith, and Debra Fiori at Parsons; Bob Carrigan and Josh Peirez, both of whom I first met at DnB; Telisa Yancy at

American Family; Sergey Young at Invest AG; Shao-Lee Lin, who I first met at Horizon Therapeutics; Andy Sieg and Steve Samuels at Merrill Lynch; Gil West at Delta; Anousheh Ansari at XPRIZE; Heidi Mellin at Workfront; Pat Gelsinger, Sanjay Poonen, and Betsy Sutter at VMware; at Aflac, Virgil Miller, Jamie Lee, and Rich Gilbert, whose aspirations have inspired me; the teams at Singularity University, IPP, HighGround, MentorCloud, Cornerstone, Globoforce, and Workday who are building software that help align individuals to leading without authority; my investors and supporters at Yoi; Garrett Gerson of Variant, who has helped me see how the principles of leading without authority can be applied to start-ups in their earliest stages; the team at Genesys for their partnership in building a global community of CMOs who lead without authority; the team at Edelman for their partnership in exploring the trust-building benefits of leading without authority; Kathy Mandato and her partnership to create the conference on the workforce of the future; Amanda Hodges at Dell who has recognized the need for leading without authority among CIOs; Vishen Lakhiani of MindValley who offered us a platform to evangelize to the broadest audience; and David Wilkie of World 50, where I learned so much years ago as a CMO member, and where I have continued to grow and learn from my friends there.

This book is the result of many years of conversations with so many people I consider my partners in thought leadership, among them my good friend Peter Diamandis, my coach Sean McFarland, and friends and fellow authors Morrie Shechtman, Adam Grant, Jim Collins, Kim Scott, Brené Brown, and Amy Edmondson.

I also need to thank so many of my own teammates along the way who have gone along with me on the roller-coaster ride of my development as a leader. They include the earliest of bosses and mentors, like Greg Seal, who now sits on the Ferrazzi Greenlight board, to my teammate Jim Hannon, who got it from the very beginning when I didn't get it myself, and friends and outside advisors like Ray Gallo and Pierre-Olivier Garcin and Eric Pulier, who continue to hang in there with me as I do my best to grow into the kind of leader exemplified in this book.

The manuscript began sometime in 2014, and I am very grateful to the writers who helped me develop my ideas over the subsequent years, including Tahl Raz, Annie Brunholzl, Amanda Ibey, Dennis Kneale, and Gali Kronenberg. Much of what appears here has been shaped by the valuable insights provided by a large number of friends who served as volunteer test readers. I am so grateful for their generous feedback!

For their generous direct contributions to the book, I am grateful to all the leaders *with* authority whose thoughtful quotations run throughout these pages. Thanks also to Tony Telschow and Nik Nadeau at Target and Jerry Dombrowski at Merrill Lynch for their added assistance with the manuscript.

I am deeply grateful to my literary agent, Esmond Harmsworth at Aevitas Creative Management, for his unyielding support, wise counsel, and brilliant editorial comments every step of the way, and to my writing partner, Noel Weyrich, who helped me tie everything together and bring the manuscript home. Thanks to Talia Krohn and her entire team at Random House for their care, advice, and commitment to excellence throughout the publishing process.

And a special word of thanks to Roger Scholl, who retired as executive editor of the Crown Publishing Group in 2019, just after providing his final masterful touches on this manuscript. Roger changed my life back in 2003 when he read a magazine interview I'd given and phoned me out of the blue to suggest I write a book for him. That book, *Never Eat Alone,* became a *New York Times* bestseller. It was a truly life-changing experience that gave me and Ferrazzi Greenlight the profound privilege to serve millions of people all over the world. Years later it is responsible for so much of who I am today. It's been a true dream, and it all started with Roger, who saw something that I did not see in myself. I will remain forever deeply and emotionally grateful for his partnership over these past sixteen years.

Finally, I want to express my gratitude to the hundreds of thousands of associates around the world that my team and I at Ferrazzi Greenlight have been privileged to work with. Some of the stories of their travails and triumphs are told in this book, with pseudonyms to preserve their anonymity. I've been inspired watching these leaders adapt to the exponential pace of change that has engulfed business today. I have been in awe, more often than not, at their passion and determination to rise to the challenge, to learn, to grow, and to be better leaders. I truly believe they will lead this world to a brighter future as we all co-elevate and go higher together.

notes

Introduction: The New Work Rules for a New Work World

1. Keith Ferrazzi and Tahl Raz, *Never Eat Alone: And Other Secrets to Success, One Relationship at a Time* (New York: Crown Business, 2005).
2. Deloitte, "Human Capital Trends 2016," deloitte.com/us/en/insights/focus/human-capital-trends/2016/identifying-future-business-leaders-leadership.html.
3. thrive.dxc.technology/2019/03/05/how-we-will-work-in-2028-gartner/r.
4. Klaus Schwab and Nicholas Davis, *Shaping the Future of the Fourth Industrial Revolution* (New York: Currency, 2018).
5. Deloitte, "Human Capital Trends 2016," deloitte.com/us/en/insights/focus/human-capital-trends/2016/human-capital-trends-introduction.html.
6. Dwight D. Eisenhower, quotes on Leadership & Organization, Eisenhower Foundation, dwightdeisenhower.com/190/Leadership-Organization.
7. Raymond Kurzweil, "The Law of Accelerating Concerns," Kurzweil: Accelerating Intelligence, March 7, 2001, kurzweilai.net/the-law-of-accelerating-returns.
8. Peter H. Diamandis and Steven Kotler, *Abundance: The Future Is Better Than You Think* (New York: Free Press, 2012).

Rule Two: Accept That It's *All* on You

1. Cheryl Bachelder, *Dare to Serve: How to Drive Superior Results by Serving Others* (Oakland, Calif.: Berrett-Koehler Publishers, 2018).
2. Richard Karlgaard and Michael S. Malone, *Team Genius: The New Science of High-Performing Organizations* (New York: Harper Business, 2015).
3. seths.blog/2013/01/out-on-a-limb.
4. cosmosmagazine.com/biology/social-rejection-and-physical-pain -are-linked.
5. Jocko Willink, *Extreme Ownership: How U.S. Navy SEALs Lead and Win* (New York: St. Martin's Press, 2015).
6. ethicsunwrapped.utexas.edu/glossary/fundamental-attribution -error.

Rule Three: Earn Permission to Lead

1. Author's note: The Landmark Forum's programming comes from Werner Erhard's popular 1970s program EST, a controversial self-help seminar in which, despite the knocks against it, I found a few valuable insights that have shaped how I approach relationships.
2. Adam M. Grant, *Give and Take: Why Helping Others Drives Our Success* (New York: Penguin Books, 2014).
3. Grant, *Give and Take*, p. 258.
4. Grant, *Give and Take*, p. 15.
5. sdbullion.com/blog/how-much-platinum-is-in-the-world.
6. news.gallup.com/poll/241649/employee-engagement-rise.aspx.
7. nytimes.com/2014/06/01/opinion/sunday/why-you-hate-work .html?_r=1.
8. Brené Brown, *Daring Greatly: How the Courage to Be Vulnerable Transforms the Way We Live, Love, Parent, and Lead* (New York: Avery, 2015).

Rule Four: Create Deeper, Richer, More Collaborative Partnerships

1. thestreet.com/story/13959499/1/sell-target-stock-on-weak-holiday -sales-amazon-competition-goldman.html.
2. marketwatch.com/story/target-suffers-record-stock-price-plunge -2017-02-28.
3. money.usnews.com/investing/stock-market-news/articles/2019-08 -21/target-corporation-tgt-stock-jumps-to-an-all-time-high.
4. barrons.com/articles/as-stock-indexes-hit-record-heights -guggenheims-minerd-says-were-near-a-minsky-moment-and-silly -season-in-risk-assets-2019-12-23.
5. fool.com/investing/2017/08/21/how-target-plans-to-replace-10 -billion-in-sales.aspx.

6. cultofmac.com/475449/tim-cook-says-diversity-key-apples-magical-products.

7. reuters.com/article/us-target-results/target-posts-best-comparable-sales-growth-in-13-years-shares-hit-record-idUSKCN1L712Q.

8. fool.com/earnings/call-transcripts/2018/11/20/target-corporation-tgt-q3-2018-earnings-conference.aspx.

9. fastcompany.com/most-innovative-companies/2019.

10. fastcompany.com/company/target.

11. statista.com/chart/20386/guests-staying-at-airbnb-appartments-on-new-years-eve.

12. vox.com/2019/3/25/18276296/airbnb-hotels-hilton-marriott-us-spending.

13. wsj.com/articles/marriott-completes-acquisition-of-starwood-hotels-resorts-1474605000.

14. Ray Dalio, *Principles* (New York: Simon & Schuster, 2017), p. 321.

15. annualreviews.org/doi/pdf/10.1146/annurev-orgpsych-031413-091305.

16. annualreviews.org/doi/pdf/10.1146/annurev-orgpsych-031413-091305.

17. Julia Rozovsky, "The Five Keys to a Successful Google Team," Google, November 17, 2015, accessed April 12, 2018, rework.withgoogle.com/blog/five-keys-to-a-successful-google-team/.

18. Rozovsky, "The Five Keys to a Successful Google Team."

19. sciencedirect.com/topics/psychology/emotional-contagion.

20. Francesca Gino, "The Business Case for Curiosity," *Harvard Business Review,* September–October 2018, p. 48.

21. cbsnews.com/news/delta-air-lines-rises-to-top-of-annual-u-s-airline-ranking/.

Rule Five: Co-Development

1. Kim Scott, *Radical Candor: Be a Kick-Ass Boss Without Losing Your Humanity* (New York: St. Martin's Press, 2019).

2. Marcia Reynolds, *The Discomfort Zone: How Leaders Turn Difficult Conversations into Breakthroughs* (Williston, Vt.: Berrett-Koehler Publishers, 2014).

3. Alexandra Sifferlin, "Is Your Cell Phone Making You a Jerk?" *Time,* February 20, 2012, healthland.time.com/2012/02/20/is-your-cell-phone-making-you-a-jerk/.

4. fortune.com/2014/10/29/ceo-best-advice/.

Rule Six: Praise and Celebrate

1. thecut.com/2016/08/how-to-motivate-employees-give-them -compliments-and-pizza.html.
2. Carlos A. Estrada, Alice M. Isen, and Mark J. Young, "Positive Affect Facilitates Integration of Information and Decreases Anchoring in Reasoning among Physicians," *Organizational Behavior and Human Decision Processes* 72, no. 1 (October 1997): 117–35, academia.edu/ 11274527/Positive_Affect_Facilitates_Integration_of_Information _and_Decreases_Anchoring_in_Reasoning_among_Physicians.
3. Estrada, et al., "Positive Affect," p. 129.
4. Estrada, et al., "Positive Affect," p. 129.
5. "Michael Lewis on Character Building and 'Coach,'" NPR, June 11, 2005, npr.org/templates/story/story.php?storyId=4699508.
6. O.C. Tanner Learning Group White Paper, "Performance: Accelerated," p. 3, octanner.com/content/dam/oc-tanner/documents/ global-research/White_Paper_Performance_Accelerated.pdf.
7. O.C. Tanner Learning Group White Paper, "Performance: Accelerated."
8. Lisa Firestone, PhD, "The Healing Power of Gratitude: The Many Ways Being Grateful Benefits Us," *Psychology Today*, November 19, 2015.
9. hult.edu/blog/celebrate-failure-not-just-success.
10. Interview with Henry Blodgett, Business Insider, December 2, 2014, youtube.com/watch?v=Xx92bUw7WX8.
11. Ibid.
12. wd40company.com/our-company/our-history.
13. tribe.wd40company.com/our-tribe/learning-teaching.
14. appel.nasa.gov/2010/02/25/ao_1-6_f_mistakes-html.

Rule Seven: Co-Elevate the Tribe

1. stickk.com/tour/4.

index

about the author

KEITH FERRAZZI, founder and chairman of Ferrazzi Greenlight, has coached the world's top enterprises and most disruptive start-ups in how team transformation drives innovation and sparks business transformation. As a successful entrepreneur, thought leader, and philanthropist, he is an advocate for foster care reform and for finding new solutions to the global problems of homeless and orphaned children.

Ferrazzi is the *New York Times* #1 bestselling author of *Who's Got Your Back* and *Never Eat Alone*. His writing has also appeared in *The Wall Street Journal, Harvard Business Review, Forbes, Fortune, Inc.* magazine, and many other leading publications. Keith is a graduate of Yale University and Harvard Business School. He lives in Los Angeles.

FerrazziGreenlight.com
KeithFerrazzi.com

about the type

This book was set in Dante, a typeface designed by Giovanni Mardersteig (1892–1977). Conceived as a private type for the Officina Bodoni in Verona, Italy, Dante was originally cut only for hand composition by Charles Malin, the famous Parisian punch cutter, between 1946 and 1952. Its first use was in an edition of Boccaccio's *Trattatello in laude di Dante* that appeared in 1954. The Monotype Corporation's version of Dante followed in 1957. Though modeled on the Aldine type used for Pietro Cardinal Bembo's treatise *De Aetna* in 1495, Dante is a thoroughly modern interpretation of that venerable face.

Available from *New York Times* bestselling author
KEITH FERRAZZI

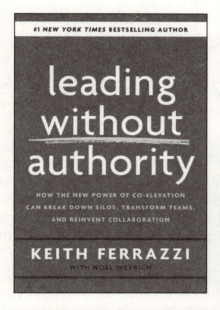
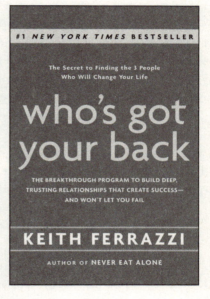
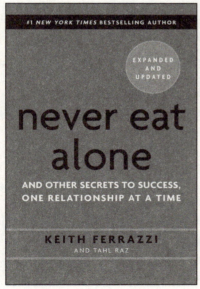

FERRAZZI GREENLIGHT

TRANSFORMING TEAMS TO TRANSFORM THE WORLD

Do you want your team to co-elevate®?

Guided by a mission to transform teams to transform the world, Ferrazzi Greenlight pioneered the practice of executive team coaching. Over the course of more than a decade partnering with many of the most prominent teams and organizations in the world, Ferrazzi Greenlight developed a proven methodology for team transformation. Today, this proven methodology is available to anyone who wants to create a High-Impact Team.

High-Impact Teams are differentiated by the way they work and the outcomes they achieve. Members break down silos and engage in deep, inclusive collaboration that yields breakthrough innovations and creative solutions through the power of co-elevation.

Ferrazzi Greenlight has empowered High-Impact Teams to accelerate key business outcomes and win in the marketplace, achieving unparalleled results including:

- **21-point increase in share price**
- **Helping struggling startups successfully pivot and thrive through crisis**
- **Rebounding from bankruptcy to profitability in record time**
- **Drastically exceeding private equity expectations**
- **Smashing new records of revenue and profitability**

Discover how your team can co-elevate to better results by visiting

FerrazziGreenlight.com

Keith Ferrazzi

G O I N G   H I G H E R   T O G E T H E R

Keith Ferrazzi is the author of the #1 *New York Times* bestsellers *Who's Got Your Back* and *Never Eat Alone*. He is the founder and chairman of Ferrazzi Greenlight, an entrepreneur, and a coach to many of the most important executive teams in the world.

Ferrazzi was honored with the prestigious Golden Gavel award by the Toastmasters organization and recognized as one of the most creative Americans in Who's Really Who.

Ferrazzi's coaching and counsel, usually only available to the most exclusive corporations, governments, and NGOs, are now available for everyone through his highly regarded leadership courses at **FerrazziLearning.com**

To book Keith as a keynote speaker, learn more about his master classes, or book him for your leadership off-site events, please visit **KeithFerrazzi.com**